"The Easter celebration does not end with Easter Sunday. Holtz leads us gracefully through the whole season. His deceptively simple book is truly a nourishing companion for all of it. The meditations for each day are based on the author's experience and lifelong wisdom. The reader is drawn to mine the insights of his or her own stories to discover God's hand there, too. A lifelong alleluia!"

> —Irene Nowell, OSB
> Author of *Wisdom: The Good Life*
> Mount Saint Scholastica in Atchison, Kansas

"In these insightful and engaging stories, Fr. Holtz introduces us to an unforgettable cast of characters—some old friends, some chance encounters—who help him understand the many dimensions of the Easter mystery. He also encourages us to see in the faces of the people in our own lives an illumination not only of the mysteries of suffering and loss, but also of spiritual connection, redemption, and hope. What a timely gift this book is."

> —Elizabeth Wiegard, mother of student activist
> Emma González

"Fr. Albert Holtz is a good companion to have on this daily walk through the Easter season. As he shares the events in his life we learn to open our eyes to the surprises we might walk past without seeing them. He shines the light of Easter into the drama of the inner city and often, because he is open and hopeful, sees it shining back."

—Jerome Kodell, OSB
Subiaco Abbey

"Fr. Albert Holtz's reflections on *Faces of Easter* reminds us both of the homeliness and of the mystery of Easter. The many vignettes of his neighbors invite us readers to look for Christ in our own homes and neighbors. Yet each of his offerings are open-ended, requiring us to look deeper, *lectio*-style, into the moments of every day, willing to be surprised and welcomed by the risen Christ known by faith and encountered anew here and now. Fr. Albert is willing to share his own vulnerability and growing edges, which in turn encourages us to accept our own."

—Norvene Vest, OblSB
Author of *Preferring Christ, a Devotional Commentary on the Rule of St. Benedict*

FACES OF EASTER

*Meeting the Paschal Mystery
in the People Around Us*

Albert Holtz, OSB

Illustrations by Daniel Partain

LITURGICAL PRESS
Collegeville, Minnesota

www.litpress.org

Library of Congress Cataloging-in-Publication Data

Names: Holtz, Albert, author.
Title: Faces of Easter : meeting the Paschal mystery in the people around us / Albert Holtz, OSB ; illustrations by Daniel Partain.
Description: Collegeville, Minnesota : Liturgical Press, 2019.
Identifiers: LCCN 2018026412 (print) | LCCN 2018043966 (ebook) | ISBN 9780814684900 (ebook) | ISBN 9780814684658
Subjects: LCSH: Eastertide—Prayers and devotions.
Classification: LCC BX2170.E25 (ebook) | LCC BX2170.E25 H65 2019 (print) | DDC 242/.36—dc23
LC record available at https://lccn.loc.gov/2018026412

To all my brothers and sisters

who have taught me about the Easter mystery

and whose stories fill these pages

Contents

Introduction

I guess it was when I was an altar boy in fourth grade that I first became fascinated by the solemn mysteries of Holy Week and Easter. I was drawn by the processions, the incense, the chants, and the candles and, most of all, by the beautiful story that led inevitably from the hosannas of Palm Sunday, through the horrors of Calvary to the glory of the resurrection.

Years later, I learned that there is much more to the celebration of Holy Week than merely commemorating past events or listening to stories about Jesus' life; rather, I discovered that we enter into those events as "mysteries" on the deepest, most personal level, in such a way that we experience our sufferings as part of Christ's sufferings on Calvary, and think of our own deaths as part of his dying and rising.

Identifying my sufferings with Christ's sufferings worked fine for me in theory, as long as I didn't have any personal struggles or sufferings worthy of the name. But when, as an adult, I began to experience the pains of loss and grief, I had difficulty seeing them as my sharing in Christ's passion, let alone as part of some beautiful story of God's loving plan for me. And so, like all believers, I had to

learn how to "walk by faith," and live in hope, while search-
ing all around me for any small hints of the Easter victory
that might appear among my struggles. As time goes on, I
continue to catch glimpses of the deeper dimension of the
paschal mystery in a number of different ways.

First, as a Benedictine monk, of course, I am in touch
with the paschal mystery in the daily celebration of Mass
and the Liturgy of the Hours, as you will see in some of the
following chapters. Second, I listen for the Easter message
in moments of quiet prayer and *lectio divina*, the meditative
reading of Scripture.[1]

This present book, however, reflects a third and more
down-to-earth approach: recognizing the many dimensions
of the Easter mystery every day in the people around me.
I've met the suffering Christ, for example, in a patient in
an intensive care unit, and seen Jesus rise as if from the
dead in the experience of a freshman named Walter. I've
felt the presence of Christ's Spirit in the deep prayer of a
street person named Gwendolyn, and caught a glimpse of
eternal joy in the face of a first-grader named Karim. *Faces
of Easter* shares the stories of these and many other people
who have helped me to experience more fully the meaning
of the Easter mystery.

---

1. I share some scriptural reflections on the mystery of suffering in
my book *Walking in Valleys of Darkness: A Benedictine Journey through
Troubled Times* (New York: Morehouse, 2011).

There are fifty stories, one for each day from Easter to Pentecost. Each story is followed by a reflection question if you would like to apply its lesson to your daily life. During each of the seven weeks of the Easter season, we will consider a different aspect of the Easter mystery; for example, in week one, we will look at the resurrection as our victory over death. In week two, we will reflect on human suffering as we experience it in the light of the cross. Having moved through all the weeks of Easter, we finally meet, in week seven, people with whom we experience flashes of the joy that awaits us in heaven.

So, I invite you to join me and my brothers and sisters whose stories are told here, on a journey from Easter to Pentecost. Who knows, maybe the risen Lord will decide to walk with us as well, as he walked with the two disciples on the road to Emmaus on the first Easter day, and show us how to better recognize the presence of the saving mystery of Easter in the people around us. May he walk with us not just in this holy season, but throughout our lives until that day when we see the fullness of Easter glory forever in heaven.

First Week of Easter

Victory over Death

As human beings, our greatest fear is the fear of our own deaths. According to one version of the story, death is absolute, inevitable, and terribly final. Death can be denied, or staved off for awhile, but ultimately its force brings each of us down into its awesome darkness. Christians, however, believe that the truth about death is quite different, and in fact is the very opposite of the first version.

According to the Christian story, the Good News, God took on our human flesh, becoming one of us—in the person of Jesus Christ—precisely to destroy death's power over us by dying on the cross. Then by his rising from the grave he gave us eternal life. The problem is, of course, that our own victory over death, although already won by Christ, isn't yet complete; in fact, the presence of death all around us is one of the greatest tests our faith. Still, the Good News announces that, despite appearances, the Easter event has indeed already happened, is still happening in our lives today, and will come to its triumphant conclusion in the future.

Sharing with you the stories for the first seven days after Easter (the "octave") I hope to introduce you to people who live the Good News by confronting death with courage and hope, and whose perspective on death is formed by Christ's Easter victory. With St. Paul, they shout confidently, "Where, O death, is your victory?" (1 Cor 15:55).

Easter Sunday: *The Light of the World*

Holy Saturday night enfolds our city in deep darkness as I carry the candle high, leading the Easter Vigil procession slowly up the center aisle of the darkened church, passing the vague shapes and inky shadows of the people in the congregation; I stop halfway along to chant, "The Light of Christ," and voices respond from all around me, "Thanks be to God."

Lowering the great candle so that the servers and those closest to the flame can light their own small candles, I watch as they begin passing the "Light of Christ" along to people around them.

Then, lifting the candle high again, I continue making my way slowly up the center aisle, as the single flame is multiplied a hundred times in solemn silence, and the white walls of the church gradually begin to take on a soft yellow-orange glow, an eloquent and overpowering symbol of Christ's new life—life that conquers death itself.

I glance to my right and then to my left to watch people handing on the flame of the paschal candle in the same way our ancestors handed on the gift of faith that they had each received from believers before them, in a process that has been going on for two thousand years. Within a few minutes, the darkness in the church gives way to joyful Easter light. I like to imagine that I hear Jesus' voice saying to me, *You are the light of the world. You are the light of your brothers in the monastery, you are the light of the congregation at St. Augustine's Church at 8:30 Mass each Sunday, you are the light of the two classes of sophomores you teach each day . . .*

Once in the sanctuary, I turn and face the congregation, and marvel at the sight of two hundred flickering flames filling the building with light from wall to wall until it seems there is no place else for the flame to spread. The bright tapers form a swelling sea of light, and I realize that there is no way that the flame can be confined within the walls of St. Mary's Church.

Floating on this light, I picture hundreds of tiny flames pouring, like a river, out of the front doors of this holy place and spreading out over the whole city. I see people passing the flames up the long hill, into the new townhouses and the old crack houses, to brothers and sisters in the new stores and the old storefront churches. Thousands and thousands of Easter flames are multiplying as people pass the light along in a glorious procession around our city and beyond it into the neighboring towns and suburbs. Each person receives the flame and hurries to pass it on to friends and families, sharing the news that Christ is risen in our hearts and in our lives.

As quickly as it came, the vision fades and I am looking out at the congregation and the hundreds of small but powerful flames. And now I chant for the third and final time, on an even higher tone, "The Light of Christ"!

Voices respond to mine, but their sound seems to be coming from outside the walls as well, from every direction, from men and women, from rich and poor, from saints and sinners. The voices echo triumphantly in a shout of victory, swelling into an earth-shaking, roar: "Thanks be to God"!

Reflection

Jesus promises that he will not allow you to "remain in the dark." Have you ever felt the need to ask him to deliver you from darkness? How might you contribute to the spreading of the light of Christ in your life?

Monday of the Octave of Easter: *Walter*[1]

Here's an Easter story that truly needs to be told.

As soon as Walter walks through the door as a freshman, it's obvious that he's staggering under some heavy emotional burdens. He can't look anyone in the eye, preferring to stare at the floor instead, and if asked a question, he might not respond at all, or might mumble a monosyllable; he plods through each day, hiding behind the protective barriers he's set up and avoiding human contact as much as possible. Even shaking someone's hand seems to be an ordeal.

So, we convince him to live in our student residence hall, where he's assigned to be a member of a group of ten other kids who, like him, are dealing with serious emotional and psychological issues. The eleven have their own separate hallway in the dorm and follow a strict schedule that includes a common study hall, frequent group therapy sessions, and an individual conference once a week with one

---

1. The names of most individuals have been changed.

of our counselors. By accumulating "days" of good behavior and acceptable grades—Walter isn't particularly good at either—a student in this group can earn certain privileges, such as the right to study in his room instead of in the study hall and, eventually, to go home for a weekend visit.

The school year quickly shifts into high gear, and I have almost no contact with Walter for weeks at a time. I do hear an occasional comment from a teacher, however, that Walter is aloof and uncommunicative.

The gold light of September cools over the weeks into the grayness of December, and suddenly it's time for Christmas break, which means that Walter will be going home for the first time since the beginning of the fall semester. As all the students are charging out the door toward a two-week break, I notice Walter standing outside on the top step in front of the school, with a suitcase and a big laundry bag at his feet, peering nervously up the street. Having no idea if he'll consent to shake my hand or even acknowledge my greeting, I step out of the door and offer him my hand, saying "Have a great vacation, Walt." He ignores my hand (Had I made a mistake by offering it?), and stares at me. Then, appearing half confused, and half insulted, he looks me in the eye and asks: "What, no hug?" I stand there for a second, dumbfounded.

The moment is so full of mystery and grace and love that I won't even try to reduce it to words. But you can be sure that Walter got his hug.

Reflection

Love, as Walter found out, can transform a person. Have you experienced the grace of transformation in your life, or seen it in someone you know? If so, did the transformation require any action on your part (or the part of the person being transformed), or was it simply a gift?

Tuesday of the Octave of Easter: *Daniel*

No teenager should have to watch his mother waste away from cancer, I grumble to myself, as I drive down King Boulevard on my way to an evening memorial service for the mother of Daniel, one of my students. She has left three children, in fact. As a priest, who is called to offer comfort to people in these situations, I'm horrified by the overwhelming wrongness of it all. As I turn down another dim street, I notice the black circles of skid marks called "donuts," left by desperate teenagers in stolen cars. Right now, I'm feeling as frustrated and angry as one of those kids.

I learned as a child, one standard response to God's apparent cruelty in allowing deaths of mothers, earthquakes, suicide bombings, and SIDS. The gist of it was: *"God knows best; so just suck it up, stop complaining, and deal with it."*

I remember, even then, thinking that this couldn't be right. (Who came up with that idea, anyway?) Jesus never spoke like this in the gospels. When he sees the widow's son being carried out to be buried, does he say to the grief-stricken mother, *"Just suck it up, stop complaining, and deal with it"*? No, instead, he is moved with compassion; he walks over, stops the pallbearers before they even get to the grave, and revives the boy.

A memory flashes in me: I think of the writer, Georges Bernanos, describing a mother who, while holding her dead child in her arms, offers God a groan of exhausted resignation. Suddenly she hears the voice of God murmur gently into her ear, *"Forgive me. One day you will know, you will understand, you will thank me. But right now, what I am looking for from you is your forgiveness. Forgive me."*

In my childhood, no one had ever suggested to me that God could—or even needed to—apologize. God was, after all, perfect, incapable of making a mistake, and certainly would never need to apologize to any poor suffering sinner, including me.

But, ever since I came across that passage in Bernanos, I always enjoy introducing others, whenever I can, to this kind and gentle God who *apologizes*, who asks my pardon when I am suffering, and who promises that one day I will understand the suffering and even thank him for it. I'm still discovering more about Bernanos' God every day and have come to realize that this God who sympathizes with my suffering is the same One who suffered and died for all of us on the cross. Just how God will take the horrors of all our personal Good Fridays, and transform them into the gift of new life, our personal Easter, is still a mystery—which is why, I suppose, the Lord apologizes.

I turn up Lyons Avenue, and, peering into the descending darkness, I make out the little Baptist church, "Mount Calvary," just ahead on the left. I pull into a parking space right in front. With a heavy heart I get out of the car; I call on the risen Jesus to stand beside my young student in the throes of his grief tonight and gently whisper to his heart, *"Forgive me, Daniel. One day you will know, you will understand, you will thank me. But right now, what I am looking for from you is your forgiveness. Forgive me."*

I lock the car, turn, and slowly climb the steep steps to Mount Calvary.

Reflection

At the Last Supper Jesus warns his disciples that an hour is coming when they will be scattered, but he tells them, *"Do not let your hearts be troubled. Believe in God, believe also in me."* In the midst of their struggles the disciples' faith in a mysterious, infinitely loving God will enable them to find peace in him. Have you ever experienced some terrible calamity for which you could imagine this God apologizing?

Wednesday of the Octave of Easter:
Easter Witnesses

Fr. Bernard, our oldest monk, passed away a few days ago. Now his coffin is poised over the newly dug grave in our St. Mary's Cemetery, as a few family members and his brother monks crowd silently together under the canopy, and the rest of the mourners stand scattered on the grass among the headstones and the tall oaks.

The sight of the flower arrangements carefully placed in an effort to conceal the edges of the waiting grave makes my stomach tighten for a moment, as I picture too many open graves that, over the years, have claimed too many people who I loved. I think of my brother, especially, and, of course, my parents. Then I glance down the rows of white headstones engraved with the names of monks who taught me in school, who advised me, or showed me by their example how to live the monastic life.

The sadness gradually passes, though, as soon as the abbot invites us to pray: *"As we gather to commend our brother Bernard to God our Father and to commit his body to the earth, let us express in song and prayer our common faith in the resurrection. As Jesus Christ was raised from the dead, we too are called to follow him through death to the glory where God will be all in all."*

A truck rumbles down Springdale Avenue, oblivious to the awesome mystery unfolding nearby. Two women stop on the sidewalk and stand respectfully to watch us through the cemetery fence. I wonder what they're thinking, and what our presence here is saying to them; then I recall St. Peter claiming about himself and his fellow Christians: "we are witnesses to his resurrection!"

This morning, I think, we're walking in the footsteps of those earliest Christians, who called themselves "witnesses," and bearing witness, like them, to the reality of Christ's resurrection. Following their example and that of all our Benedictine brothers whose bodies lie at peace here, we, monks in mourning, testify to the reality of Jesus' resurrection in our lives, not just here this morning, but every hour of every day, by our lives of joyful self-giving, of quiet prayer, and of demanding work with our kids and parishioners.

We continue the graveside service. I intone Psalm 116: *"I will walk in the presence of the LORD / in the land of the living"* The sacred words carry across the yawning grave and above the headstones to reach the women on Springdale Avenue; I imagine them echoing outward toward distant graves in which my countless loved ones lie: *"Turn back, my soul, to your rest / for the LORD has been good to you; / he has kept my soul from death, / my eyes from tears . . ."*

A reading and a litany, then the abbot concludes with a final prayer: *"Into your hands, Father of mercies, we commend our brother Bernard in the sure and certain hope that, together with all who have died in Christ, he will rise with him on the last day."*

The abbot sprinkles the coffin with holy water; Fr. Bernard's ninety-year journey of witnessing on earth is finished—to be continued in heaven.

Reflection

The earliest Christians saw themselves as witnesses to Jesus' resurrection. Think of some ways that you are or could be a witness of the new life of Christ. In what places is it easiest for you to bear witness? Where is it most difficult?

Thursday of the Octave of Easter: *Rita*

I've been friends with Rita's family since teaching her daughter in high school over forty years ago, so I'm pleased that they've invited me to join them in the intensive care unit, at the bedside of ninety-two-year-old Rita. She is co-matose, and is being kept alive by a breathing machine. I stand by her bed, and gently take her hand in mine, and tell her—unconscious as she is—that I'm there praying with her.

As the twelve of us wait for Rita's ninety-year-old sister to arrive before removing the breathing machine, we listen to some Scripture readings, pray a psalm and the Litany of the Saints, all interspersed with quiet conversation, and with various family members whispering words of love into the unconscious woman's ear.

Finally, her sister arrives and joins Rita's bewildered husband at the bedside. After more hugs, tears, prayers, and whispered words of love to the dying woman, one of the granddaughters calls the nurse over and tells her that we think it's time to remove the breathing support.

As the nurse draws the privacy curtain around the bed, I stay there with Rita's husband, daughter, sons, and a few others; as they stand surrounding the bed, I move off to the side, feeling sad over losing an old friend, but joyful that she has won the final victory after a long life filled with love and kindness. My one fear is that after the breathing tube is removed, she might linger for days or weeks.

Two nurses come in and do something near the head of the bed, and within five minutes a young doctor arrives and puts his stethoscope on Rita's chest; then he turns to the nurse, and announces in a matter-of-fact tone, "Six-thirty." As the nurse dutifully jots the time on her clipboard, he walks out without another word. Wordlessly, one at a time, each of us steps up to the bed and says good-bye in our own way: a kiss on the cool forehead, a last clasp of a hand, a whispered, intimate word.

As we gather after saying our farewells to Rita, it's clear that we have finished our work here, and we slowly begin to put on our coats. I suddenly remember Luke's story of what the risen Lord does on the first Easter morning for two discouraged disciples he meets on their way home to Emmaus: for almost seven miles he journeys beside them on the road—he walks them home. And that, I think, was what we've just done with our prayers, and whispered words of love, we've "walked Rita home."

There was, of course, another person walking along with us: the same risen Lord who had accompanied the two disciples on the road to Emmaus had joined us in our prayers and in our tears. When the nurse removed the life support machine and Rita stopped breathing, our work of love was done, and we handed Rita over to the risen Jesus to walk with her the rest of the way into the kingdom of light and peace.

As we all file into the hallway, I pray that he'll be around to walk me home when the time comes.

Reflection

Have you ever been with a loved one who was near death? If so, what were your emotions? How different would the experience have been if you did not believe that you would see this person again? What does the image of "walking her home" mean to you?

Friday of the Octave of Easter: *Ernest*

Writing in a journal can be like digging with, say, a teaspoon—or with a pickaxe.

As part of a lesson on the suffering and death of Christ, I've just asked my sophomore religion students to journal with me on the question "Have you ever experienced suffering in your life, either your own suffering or the suffering of someone close to you?" Some heads rest on desks, some hands set to writing feverishly, as if to capture thoughts that are trying to escape, some eyes stare vacantly out the window, looking for lost memories.

I use my pen delicately, tentatively, like a dentist's pick, recalling and recording how I felt when my brother died many years ago. Suddenly the pen seems to morph into a pickaxe and starts plunging deep into painful, buried memories of sinking under mountainous waves of grief, and feeling as if I might never come back up. Memories of being hot with icy anger at God for allowing my brother to die at age forty-five, leaving four little children and a loving wife. I write my way quickly through those painful pieces of the past, and find myself looking back and realizing that, even in the worst moments of grief at losing my brother, I always had a sense, deep inside, that God was somehow present in all of that grief, and was standing with me, making sure that I didn't sink past the point of no return. I had, I note on the page, an undefined sense that I was not alone.

Time is up. The students start sharing their journal entries out loud: a torn ligament, the death of a grandmother, and other painful slices of normal adolescence.

"I want to say something about suffering." The gentle whisper is Ernest. He has had far more than his fair share of struggles in his life and gets help from one of our school's counselors a couple of times a week. An expectant silence sets in.

"When you've been abused by members of your family," he begins, "and kids at school laugh at you behind your back," (a couple of his classmates look away, embarrassed) "and you think nobody cares about you, that's suffering!" His soft, calm voice imposes itself on the room as everyone waits, curious to see if he has more to say.

"Twice this past year, my suffering got so bad that I stood on the platform at Penn Station and came this close to throwing myself under a train." He holds up his right hand, with the thumb and forefinger almost touching, turning slowly to show the half-inch gap between his fingers to everyone in the room. He whispers in a voice suddenly shaking with emotion, "I swear to God—this close!" Dead silence. Then his final whisper, "I felt all alone."

His classmates are sitting perfectly still, some watching him intently, others staring uneasily at their hands folded on their desks.

"I felt all alone." My heart goes out to him, and I remember what I just wrote in my journal, how once, when my suffering seemed almost unbearable, some hidden part of me, deep down, knew that I was not alone. I wish that I could share that spark of hope with him right now, but I'll have to wait until after class. I speak silently to him:

Ernest, you weren't alone; Jesus, the one who rose victorious from the dead, was right beside you, helping you to stare down death itself, and coaxing you to step back from the edge of the railroad platform—twice!

The normally boisterous classroom is as quiet as death—Ernest's story is a tough act to follow.

Reflection

Do you ever connect your own sufferings with those of Christ on the cross? If so, what difference does this make? If not, you might reflect on St. Paul's words to the Romans:

"[I]t is that very Spirit bearing witness with our spirit that we are children of God, and if children, then heirs, heirs of God and joint heirs with Christ—if, in fact, we suffer with him so that we may also be glorified with him" (Rom 8:16-17).

Saturday of the Octave of Easter:
Sorrowful Mothers

Okay, so we all know that Christ's victory over the power of death at Easter is far from complete, and we know that we're waiting for him to return one day to finish the job. But we also know that waiting for that day can test our faith to the breaking point. Here's a "Christmas story" that offers an Easter message.

As soon as I slip into a seat near the back of our school auditorium the evening after our school's joyful Christmas program, I feel an ironic contradiction. It's now only two days before Christmas, but I'm attending a vigil service for the dozen young men who have died as victims of violence in our city during the last few months. I feel overwhelmed by the irony.

A Baptist minister on stage bemoans the continual senseless killing of our city's young men, and after speaking a few words of comfort to the grieving families, returns to his seat among the several other clergymen, next to the mayor. The contradiction weighs more and more heavily on me: less than twenty-four hours ago I stood on that stage conducting a sixty-voice chorus in our annual school Christmas program—a service of readings, songs, instrumental music, and slides that celebrates the life of Jesus from Christmas to his final coming at the end of time as "King of Kings." Now, death seems to be directing tonight's program, and my sense of joy and accomplishment fades away.

In place of last night's proclamation of God's victory over death and sin, tonight's mistress of ceremonies intones, very slowly, the names of twelve murdered young people. When she reads a name, a woman—presumably the mother—from that victim's family comes up onto the stage to receive a small bouquet of roses, and then returns solemnly to her seat.

I stare at the bright red cloth decorating the podium, and the several poinsettias left from last night's joyful event. And I remember the powerful voices and the blare of trumpets during the triumphant finale as the energetic

Christmas choir celebrated the Lord's final coming: *"He's the King of Kings, He's the Lord of Lords! He's the Master of Everything! Let him be adored!"*

Here, on the next evening, the somber voice of the mistress of ceremonies grates in my thoughts against last night's chorus and the jubilant brass section. With each name she reads and each bouquet the mayor presents, the mood grows darker and my heart heavier.

Nothing could be more ironic: as she accepts her bouquet, each mother who has lost a son walks past the Christmas poinsettias that celebrated the birth of a son to a young mother in Bethlehem. The tragic parade continues relentlessly. This evening, Good Friday has replaced Christmas. The red flowers and the red hanging that proclaimed Christ's birth and his total victory last night are no longer a joyful Christmas crimson, but seem to have turned martyrs' red, the color of teenagers' blood spilled and splashed on our city's streets.

My heart aches for the twelve heartbroken women bearing their heavy bouquets. For them, the promised King of Kings is already too late in coming, and they have nothing left but those terrible flowers that reflect the permanent scars of grief and loss.

After the program is over, and I'm left alone in the quiet, empty auditorium, I trudge up onto the stage to take down the bright Christmas hanging from the podium. I stop and study the poinsettias, wondering what they'll look like in the sanctuary during tomorrow night's midnight Mass.

Will they become Christmas flowers again, or will they remain mournful reminders to me of the blood of young people who died before the King could return?

Reflection

If Christianity is full of contrasts, nowhere is this more obvious than in the paschal mystery, where death leads to life and defeat turns into to victory. Think of some times in your life when you had to share in Christ's suffering. Was it possible at the time to see the experience as part of God's redemptive plan, as something leading ultimately to victory and eternal life? If not, what did you do in the face of the defeat?

Second Week of Easter

Sharing in the Cross

One essential insight into the Easter mystery is that, through the merits of Jesus' passion and cross, our own suffering is mysteriously transformed into the very means of our salvation, and takes on meaning, purpose, and eternal significance. This week's chapters explore some of the ways we share in the cross of the crucified and risen Christ through the sufferings and struggles of our daily lives.

Second Sunday of Easter: *The Artist*

Now, I'm not saying that my mom intended to teach us theology when I was five years old; she simply liked to draw for us when we asked her to. But, I certainly felt something deeper going on when my brother and sister and I would ask her to make us a sketch.

She sits down at the kitchen table, and we crowd close around her, craning our necks, waiting for the magic to start. Suddenly, countless quick lines begin to pour from her pencil onto the paper, looking at first like threads for a spider web; then they quickly arrange themselves as if by magic, into a nose, a pair of eyes, a mouth. We stand mute, entranced. We never tire of watching this almost divine trick: she can create people out of nothing. But that's not the theology part—that comes next.

After the outline of the sketch is completed, she goes back to fill in the shadows. Her trained artist's hand swiftly darkens the right areas until, one after another, the parts of the flat, two-dimensional figure start to come to life: the head becomes round, the eyes sink into their sockets (I stare at them, willing them to blink), the lips become full, the nose stands out from the rounded cheeks. A powerful, warm sense of satisfaction always floods me whenever I watch the dark parts make the sketch complete.

Mind you, I was a pretty typical kid. I liked playing catch and riding on swings and playing in dirt and rummaging through my oldest brother's private stuff, and I didn't know much about pain and suffering and evil. Yet

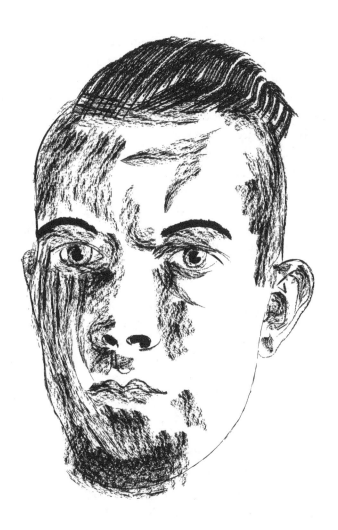

I knew instinctively that there was something mysterious and beautiful in the way the shadows caused the rest of the drawing to come to life. And each time I watched my mother draw, the lesson sank in a little deeper: the dark parts are the important secret ingredient of reality, they give it a quality it wouldn't otherwise have.

That was decades ago. Sorrows and sins and suffering have drawn plenty of dark lines into the drawing that is me, and the agony of grief has etched shadows against the joy, the love, and the satisfaction that have characterized my life. Part of me still stands at the kitchen table, marveling at the way the Artist uses mysterious black shadows to shape me into the person the Lord wants me to be.

Reflection

If you think of your life as a pencil drawing, what might be the blackest lines and the shadowy parts? Do you have a sense as to the purpose or significance of these dark areas of your life? What emotions do you feel when looking at the dark parts of your life's story? How might those experiences fit into the Easter mystery?

Monday of the Second Week of Easter:
The Film Editor

Here's a lesson that might be useful the next time trials and tragedies start to overwhelm you. I learned it while watching a ninety-minute documentary about our monastery and school.

I'm amazed at how cleverly the filmmaker has taken the hours he's spent interviewing me, and, by editing out every hesitation, clumsy phrase, repetition, and digression, has transformed the rambling interviews into a couple of smoothly flowing monologues. He's made it seem as if I naturally speak in long, coherent paragraphs that flow easily from one idea to the next. Even *I* am impressed with this edited version of Fr. Albert!

As I watch myself on the screen, I begin to think of the great power that a film editor exercises: he starts with the raw film footage, but then he shapes people into heroes or cowards, and decides whether the story will end miserably or happily.

Then I ask myself: what if I could take the story of my life and edit out certain negative or painful episodes? It seems like such a good idea that I start to make a list of bad things I would drop. First on my list of horrible experiences to edit out is the horror of watching our prep school close in 1972. In the space of a couple of months, I saw all of my hopes and plans for the future completely vanish, leaving me devastated and brokenhearted. I would gladly erase that painful episode from my life.

Meanwhile, on the screen, the documentary has moved past that early period of worry and uncertainty, past the re-opening of St. Benedict's Prep a year after its tragic closing, and is now describing the school in its present form. It shows several students sitting in a circle with a school counselor and talking about their personal struggles: one student has never met his father, another lives with a drug-addicted mother, and so on. These teenagers are learning that the best thing to do about their problems is to face them squarely, even if this is sometimes very difficult to do. I see in their faces and body language that some of them are already growing stronger by honestly admitting their troubles and then struggling to overcome them.

As I watch these courageous kids in the counseling group, though, my personal life-editing project hits a snag: if I leave out the "death" of St. Benedict's Prep in 1972, then the school we're seeing on the screen will never be born, and these kids will never have the opportunity to sit in that room and wrestle with their problems. This editing process has suddenly become a lot more complicated than I expected: it was only the painful closing of St. Benedict's in 1972 that made it possible for the school to rise, as if from the dead, to a unique, exciting new life. I quickly realize that God had been using all of those difficult moments and painful experiences as opportunities to shape us monks, to help us grow, and to bring about new life in our monastery, our school—and me.

As the film ends and the lights come on, I conclude that it's just as well that God hasn't given me editing privileges over the events in my life's story.

Reflection
The mystery of suffering isn't some painful glitch in the unfolding story of God's love for me; the cross is right at the center. Can you think of an instance when the mystery of Jesus' victory resulting from defeat has shown itself

in your life? What did that experience feel like? What, if anything, did you learn from it?

Tuesday of the Second Week of Easter:
Mary Ann

In my black suit and Roman collar, I stare at the pale, unconscious stranger lying on a bed in the ICU, connected to an intravenous drip and two monitors. When I finally recognize Mary Ann as the stranger in the bed, I swallow against the lump in my throat. She has been my friend for over forty years.

A solemn, uneasy silence settles down on her husband Don and me as we face one another on either side of the bed, and grapple with the unspoken truth that Mary Ann might die within the next few days or hours.

When she stirs in her sleep, Don tells her that I'm here for a visit. I bend over and gently whisper hello, not knowing if she can hear me from the depths of wherever she is. Her eyes open into slits: a look of recognition, an exhausted smile, and then a plunge back into the depths. I glance up at the mysterious green graphs and numbers glowing on the monitors, and then at Don's exhausted, tense face. I stifle a deep sigh as I look up quickly toward the ceiling so that my tears won't show.

But suddenly I feel something else growing in my heart besides sadness: an overwhelming sense of awe. The three of us in this ICU room are in the presence of a deep, unfathomable mystery. Without realizing that I'm speaking out loud, I whisper to myself, "Well, we're certainly on holy ground here!" To my surprise, Don nods in agreement and adds, "We sure are."

He seems to understand that I'm repeating the Lord's words to Moses, who was walking over for a closer look at the mysterious burning bush: *"Come no closer! Remove the sandals from your feet, for the place on which you are standing is holy ground"* (Exod 3:5). Moses had wandered into the presence of an awesome power far beyond his human limitations, a mystery so deep that it needed to be approached reverently, in bare feet.

As I stand at the bedside, I can feel that the three of us, too, are in the presence of an awesome power far beyond our ability to comprehend or explain: the deep mystery of human suffering, and God's presence in it. Amid the beeping monitors and intravenous tubes, we are indeed on holy ground.

I open my book of prayers for the sick, and, in a voice trembling with a mixture of love and hope and sadness, read God's words spoken through Isaiah: *"Do not fear: I am with you; / do not be anxious: I am your God. / I will strengthen you, I will help you, / I will uphold you with my victorious right hand"* (Isa 41:10, NABRE).

I don't suppose that Mary Ann can hear me, so I read for Don—and for myself. At the end of the reading, I say, *"The word of the Lord."* As Don answers with the traditional response, I see Mary Ann's lips form the words along with her husband: *"Thanks be to God."* I smile—her whispered response reassures me that, even from the depths of semiconsciousness, my friend has been listening to those comforting words, *"Do not fear: I am with you . . ."* She knows: her suffering has brought her into a mysterious place—holy ground.

Reflection

Suffering comes in many forms—physical, emotional, psychological. Have you ever felt that you were on "holy ground" in the presence of the mystery of suffering? Did you sense that the risen Christ was somehow present as well?

Wednesday of the Second Week of Easter: *The Throng*

This is my favorite prayer time of the week, the Saturday night "service of light" that leads into Vigils of Sunday. The monks are standing in the rear of the church, a circle of black, shadowy figures, gathered around the tall paschal candle, our faces dimly lit by its flame. Fr. Augustine lifts the candle out of its stand and, with a brother walking at either side holding a lighted taper, leads the procession up the center aisle of the darkened church. As we walk in the dark, following the flame that is the light of Christ, I begin singing:

Longing for light, we wait in darkness. Longing for truth, we turn to you.

Make us your own, your holy people, light for the world to see.

The "Service of Light" is a prayer for a victory that is still to come: the final, complete victory of light over darkness, of our Savior's cross over the powers of sin and death. All of the monks in the procession join me in the chorus:

Christ, be our light! Shine in our hearts. Shine through the darkness.

Christ, be our light! Shine in your Church gathered today.
Squinting against the glare of my candle, I sing,
Longing for food, many are hungry . . .

"Longing for food . . ." The dozens of people "longing for food," who lined up in a humble procession on the sidewalk in front of the monastery's food pantry this morning are now walking alongside us.

Longing for peace, our world is troubled . . . [1]

"Our world is troubled . . ." Sixteen missing teens (I counted them) whose pictures I studied at the post office yesterday fall in behind me. Then thousands of persecuted Christians in Syria join us, then thousands of Chinese political prisoners, and thousands of children from refugee camps in Africa—we are now what the Bible calls a "throng." The flame of the paschal candle at the head of the procession shines bright and strong, with the infinite power of Christ, although—and this is the whole point of our light service—his victory over darkness and despair is still far from complete.

In a few minutes, at Vigils, we'll celebrate our certainty that, by rising from the dead, Christ has already won the

---

1. Bernadette Farrell, "Christ, Be Our Light!," (Portland: OCP, 2000).

battle: but right now, we walk toward our choir stalls in darkness, sharing the sadness of all of suffering humanity, and crying out, *"Christ, be our light!"*

The throng reaches the choir stalls, which are still in almost total darkness. Fr. Augustine lifts the paschal candle high onto a stand in the center of the wide aisle between the two facing rows of choir stalls, where the candle seems to be shining brighter and brighter, and we end with a prayer:

"Lord God, whose Son, our Savior Jesus Christ, triumphed over death and prepared for us a place in the new Jerusalem, grant that we who gather to give thanks for his resurrection may praise you in that city of which he is the Light, and where he lives for ever and ever."[2]

"Amen!" rises from the throng and resounds through the vastness of the church, along with the prayer of every sister and brother in the world who is also longing for the light.

Reflection

The processional song sang *of "Longing for light . . . longing for food . . . longing for peace . . ."* Can you think of some longings in your heart that remind you that you are incomplete, and that you need to fill up that incompleteness with God? Think of some of the longings of our brothers and sisters that are evident in recent news stories.

---

2. Daily Evening Prayer, Rite 2, collect for Sundays, in *Book of Common Prayer* (New York: Church Hymnal).

Thursday of the Second Week of Easter: *Willie*

Sometimes the Lord gives us creative ways of coping with our problems. Willie found a good one last spring.

Thirty freshmen crowd onto a patch of grass outside a classroom building and share the five trees as they practice tying knots while their sophomore camping instructors walk around offering advice. In a couple of weeks, when the freshmen are on their fifty-three-mile backpacking hike along the New Jersey section of the Appalachian Trail, today's lesson will be useful: it involves learning how to tie both a slipknot and a Siberian hitch.

I walk slowly over to a freshman named Willie, who has so many struggles in his life that he's always getting himself in trouble in school, and I throw down a friendly challenge: "Okay, Willie, tie me a Siberian hitch around that tree!" His eyes brighten as he grabs his five feet of yellow practice rope and sets to work with determination and concentration. In no time, he has the knot done correctly and turns to me, eager for my approval.

"Whoa!" I cheer, loud enough for those around us to hear, "Way to go with the Siberian hitch, man!"

"Wait! Lemme show you a slipknot, Father Al! Hold on."

It's obvious that Willie, not the strongest of students in the classroom, to put it mildly, wants to show anyone who is willing to watch, that he has mastered something.

"Okay, go for it!"

I watch as he talks to his fingers, whispering instructions about each next step. The slipknot is soon done well enough to rate another approving word from me: "Willie's goin' all crazy tyin' these knots!" I shout, to the amusement of his classmates. His wide smile shows his satisfaction over having conquered the slipknot and the Siberian hitch.

As I look at his knot tied snugly around the rough trunk of the tree, I realize that he has a lot of knots in his life: beginning with his absent parents and the fact that he hasn't spent a full semester in any one school for years, his life is full of the snarls and snags of suffering and unsolvable situations.

When the future Pope Francis was still Jorge Mario Bergoglio and studying in Germany, he came across a Bavarian painting of the Virgin Mary that showed her serenely untying knots in a long white ribbon. It was called *Maria Knotenlöserin*, "Mary, Undoer of Knots." He was so touched by the image that he bought a copy of the painting, took it home to Argentina, and started promoting devotion to Mary under this title.

The kids work on their Siberian hitches with varying degrees of success, and Willie is teaching a teammate how to improve his knot-tying technique. Willie loves just tying and untying that knot over and over, as if, by mastering that knot, he's wrestling successfully with some of the tight knots that bind up his life. Perhaps his feeling of success is actually loosening the grip of his own knots just a little bit, at least for a few moments.

Maybe the reason Willie loves the Siberian hitch so much is simply that he can untie it with one quick tug. He can undo each knot instantly, with just a simple snap of his wrist, with no complicated untying or problem-solving to go through. There's probably something appealing about that. But his life-knots won't come undone quite as easily as a Siberian hitch.

Wouldn't it be cool if, since his own mother is unable to take care of him, he might be adopted as a favorite son by Mary, the Undoer of Knots?

Reflection

Can you think of one particular knot in your life that finally was untied? Can you see how God may have been involved in unloosening it? Are you experiencing any difficult "knots" at the moment that you might present to Christ—or to Mary, the Undoer of Knots?

Friday of the Second Week of Easter:
The Day Hiker

A yellow sign in big black letters warns, "You Are in Bear Country." I glance fearfully over each shoulder, but see only the empty campsite ringed by towering trees and thickets of mountain laurel—no bears in sight.

I turn and squint up at the smaller print: "Store all food in bear proof containers," "Never run from a bear," "Make noise on the trail," and several more rules for how to handle yourself when in bear country.

You hear people joke that their home state is "God's country." But what if you actually took seriously the idea that you live in "God's country?" Imagine a big yellow sign with black letters declaring, "You Are in God's Country!"

The Israelites of the Old Testament knew all about being in "God's country"—they called it "the wilderness." For forty years, they trekked in that trackless terrain that was untamed, unmapped, filled with dangers from snakes and hostile tribes, with no roads or any other traces of human habitation. They didn't need any yellow signs on trees to tell them that the territory they were in was not theirs but "God's country." The wilderness was a place where all of their strength and brainpower counted for nothing—humans were simply not in control there. They depended on God for everything: food, water, and protection from hostile tribes. The wilderness was a symbol of the mystery of God.

I've been in that kind of wilderness, "God's country," a couple of times, and had to confront the mystery of God up close—way too close. When our monastery's school abruptly closed its doors in 1972, we monks found ourselves in unmapped, trackless terrain filled, for all we knew, with deadly perils lying in wait for us in the darkness. Despite all of our discussions and planning meetings, I spent many anxious, sleepless nights agonizing over the unknown future. Although I shared the perilous time with my community, it was a grueling journey through "God's country." I still wince at the memory.

But whenever we find ourselves in the wilderness, we can read the fine print of the yellow sign that tells us how to survive in God's country: "Love the Lord your God with all your heart." "Love your neighbor as yourself." "Do not settle down and get comfortable here: you are bound for someplace else." "Put all of your trust in God alone, and not in created things." Keep reading: "Don't be a control freak." (Honest, that's what it says.) And that's a crucial bit of advice that can make all the difference in our lives.

Think about it: if we need to be in control of everything all the time, then the future (which by definition is beyond our control) is always going to be a threat. But what if we let the victorious Christ take charge? What if we trust that, by sharing in his cross and resurrection, we have already conquered, too? Ah, then everything is different: our trials and sufferings take on eternal significance—and the future is transformed from a threat into a promise.

Even when we have to walk in the wilderness at times, maybe even for long periods, at least we know that we're walking in a land where our loving God is in complete control, and where our brother, the risen, victorious Jesus, is journeying right beside us at every step—through God's country.

Reflection

Think of a "wilderness experience" of your own, when things were out of your control and you had little or no idea of what was going to happen next. What emotions did you experience? Did you pray much at the time? Did you learn any lessons about living in "God's country?" Reflect on the idea that "when we put our trust in God, the future changes from a threat to a promise."

Saturday of the Second Week of Easter: *Mina*

Ever see a girl who looks like a storm cloud? That's Mina as we sit down side by side on a bench in a quiet corner of St. Augustine's Church after Mass. Half a minute of quiet, then the cloud bursts open in a flood of tears and words. Nothing to do but wait out the storm.

"My family is moving to Illinois at the end of June . . . That means I have to leave all my friends and everything . . . I'll be in this whole new place: a new house, a sophomore in a new school where I don't know anybody."

"Scary, huh?" I ask. My heart goes out to her. She wipes tears with the heels of her hands, and tries not to sob.

"Yeah. Everything will be different. I grew up here, so I have a pretty good idea of how things work—I was even gonna try out for softball next spring, and stuff like that. But now," she shakes her black curls, "I have no idea what's gonna happen." She turns and looks at me; she's so young and seems so frail—afraid of the storm clouds gathering in front of her.

Remembering the gospel story from my morning meditation, I start to picture the two of us sitting side by side in a boat at night on the Sea of Galilee, in the midst of a raging storm. Foaming waves seem about to swamp the boat. Then she shouts, "What's that?" Peering into the gloom, I see a gray form slowly gliding toward us over the water, but I can't figure out what this strange figure is that is emerging out of the darkness. It takes on a menacing, human shape. I panic.

Then the figure calls out in a strong, soothing voice, "It is I; do not be afraid"!

And, to our surprise, he walks right past us; a moment later the boat glides smoothly onto a sandy shore, landing Mina and me safely back in our pew in the rear of St. Augustine's Church.

Mina is staring at me quizzically.

"Oh! Sorry, Mina! I was just remembering a time when I was scared, the way you are now." The two of us sit quietly, each involved in our own thoughts.

Over the years I've gotten a little better at recognizing Christ's presence more quickly in the midst of life's storms, and hearing his voice in the roar of the winds: *"It is I; do not be afraid."* But a quick look at my young boatmate reminds me that she is still a beginner when it comes to dealing with frightening lightning storms and phantom figures that glide toward one on waves, saying, *"It is I; do not be afraid."*

I try to offer her some encouraging words myself: "Okay, Mina, so what are some things you can do that might make moving to Illinois a little less scary?" I try to make my voice sound strong and soothing and, maybe, well, wise.

It's not the voice of Jesus, I admit, but it will do for now.

Reflection

A Christian tries to develop a paschal outlook on life, approaching every difficult situation with the confident conviction that the risen Lord is mysteriously present and active there, bringing about something new and good. Can you think of a time in your own life, or in the life of someone close to you, when you experienced new life arising from some painful situation?

Third Week of Easter

From Fear to Courage

Probably the most remarkable transformation in the lives of the apostles happens during the days immediately after the resurrection: their sudden change from a frightened band of followers into fearless preachers. The reason for this surprising transformation is simple: they have encountered the risen Jesus.

Today the risen Savior still gives us, his followers, hope and courage in the face of our life's challenges, transforming our doubts and fears into confidence and courage. The transformation is usually subtler than it was for the disciples who met Jesus right after the resurrection, but, as the stories that follow illustrate, there are many ways that we, too, can experience the presence of the risen Lord who tells us "Do not be afraid," and gives us hope and courage.

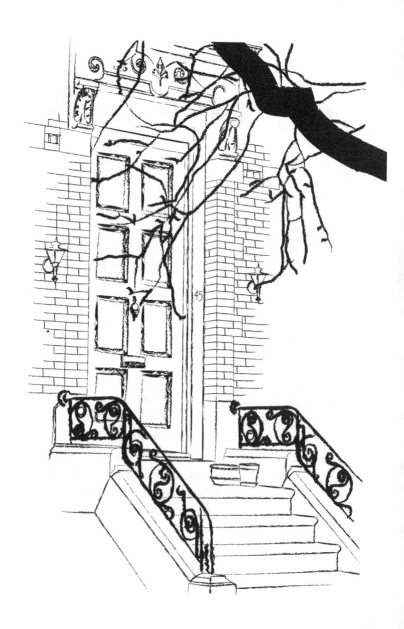

Third Sunday of Easter: *A Fearful Disciple*

Walking down James Street, not far from the monastery, past a row of restored brick rowhouses, I suddenly get this closed-in feeling. There's wrought iron grillwork protecting the windows, and most of the front doors are blank and uninviting, and fitted with tiny peepholes so that the occupants can see who is ringing their bell.

The iron-grilled windows and the sealed-up doors remind me of the gospel passage we heard on Easter—the story of the twelve apostles on the first Easter Sunday evening. They were hiding behind a locked door like one of these, afraid that the authorities were about to come and arrest them. I can imagine them staring anxiously at the door, sneaking glances at one another, expecting at any moment to hear the fateful knock that would signal arrest, torture, and death. Then, just as the suspense becomes unbearable, they see the risen Jesus standing in their midst, greeting them: "Peace be with you."

Further along James Street, the wrought iron bars on a window catch my eye. When I slow my pace to study them closely, I suddenly feel uneasy for some reason that I can't put my finger on. Then, as I keep staring, I realize that sometimes my own heart and soul must look like that. When I'm in a situation where I'm not in control, or where I'm not sure what's going to happen next, or I feel threatened, then up go my defenses—locked doors, closed shutters, iron bars, the works.

Too often I even put up defenses against God, afraid that he'll ask too much of me—that is, challenge me to shift the center of my life from myself to him. So, when the Lord wants to come and meet me or teach me some difficult lesson, he has to contend with my home security system, especially my protective bars.

Luckily for me, however, Jesus doesn't seem to be put off by the barred windows and locked doors of my heart, any more than he was by that door the disciples had locked on that first Easter evening. He has lots of ways to get past my defenses. For example, I'll suddenly realize that some person has found their way into my heart despite my carefully guarded doors, I hear Jesus' loving greeting as he stands beside that person inside my defenses: *"Peace be with you"!*

I continue down the sidewalk past more sealed-up houses. A young woman is striding toward me pushing a stroller. When I glance down at the baby's serene and radiant face, I feel a tug at my heart; my breath catches as I glimpse God's glory for a moment. As mother and child continue past me, I'm about to thank Jesus for that surprise splinter of the divine presence, when I hear his voice—he's already inside my heart: *"Peace be with you"!* He's done it again.

Reflection

Do you ever find yourself putting up defenses against God? When are the times that this is most likely to happen? What are God's favorite ways of speaking to you, of getting past your defenses? Think of a time when the Lord helped you to overcome your fear, and gave you the gift of peace.

Monday of the Third Week of Easter:
The Dawn from on High

Across the street from the abbey church, someone has spray-painted a gang logo on the big electrical utility box on the corner. The logo is a grotesque notice that a certain gang has staked its claim here—and is in charge of all drug-dealing, robbery, and murder in the neighborhood—all around our monastery.

Yesterday, this logo took on undeniable reality when, one block down the hill, a man was gunned down in cold blood on the sidewalk across William Street from the abbey church, less than fifty yards from where I'm now sitting, waiting for six o'clock Morning Prayer to begin. The police told us that the victim was a notorious, violent gang member, and that his murder was inevitable.

I start to think about the endless futility of gang warfare, and of those two men, the victim and his executioner. I glance at the crucifix and notice that the body of the African Jesus nailed there in agony seems more slumped over than usual, as if he, like me, is feeling weighed down with sadness this morning.

As my brothers and I stand and begin to chant the ancient verse from Psalm 51, *"O Lord, open my lips . . . ,"* I ask the risen Jesus to give me a word of consolation during our Morning Prayer.

Now we sit and recite Psalm 24; we join in the cry of the priests and Levites as they welcome the ark of the covenant into Jerusalem: *"O gates, lift high your heads; . . . Let him enter, the king of glory!"* We monks are welcoming God into our beleaguered neighborhood right now, crossing our fingers in the hope that he will indeed agree to come in.

The psalms and readings follow one another in a peaceful half-hour procession, while a gray morning light slowly washes the darkness behind the stained-glass windows, and I keep listening in vain for that elusive word of consolation from the Lord.

At last, we stand to sing the closing canticle, the *Benedictus*—"*Blessed be the Lord, the God of Israel.*" As the great words of Zechariah disappear into the empty recesses of the church, I resign myself to the fact that there won't be any word of consolation from the Lord for me this morning. That happens sometimes.

Halfheartedly I join in chanting the final four lines of the poem: "*In the tender compassion of our God / the dawn from on high shall break upon us, / to shine on those who dwell in darkness and the shadow of death . . .*"

Finally! I hear it—the "word from the Lord" that I've been listening for since we began our Morning Prayer: "*the dawn from on high shall break upon us, / to shine on those who dwell in darkness and the shadow of death, / and to guide our feet into the way of peace.*"

In the closing lines of the last canticle of Morning Prayer, the risen Lord has reassured me that, although my brothers and I are "*dwell[ing] in darkness and the shadow of death,*" he has already conquered death through his own death and resurrection.

I glimpse a small triangle of the monastery garden through a partially open window; the rising sun has pierced night's darkness and is making the bricks of the monastery glow a bright coral red. The "Dawn from on high," is visiting us as promised, and reasserting God's sovereign claim over our neighborhood as *his* territory. God is still promising to overcome despair, drugs, and the darkness of death itself.

Reflection

Reflect on the ways that the saving mystery of the cross is present in your life, perhaps helping you to deal successfully with a problem, or encouraging you in the face of a failure of some kind. Have you ever felt the Lord shining on you in the "shadow of death?"

Tuesday of the Third Week of Easter:
Children of the Promise

Smoke swirls from the brazier in the center of the sanctuary, and rises in a column toward the high ceiling of the nave, filling the abbey church with the sweet smell of incense. The monks, standing, chant the first psalm of Sunday Vespers: *"Let my prayer arise before you like incense, / the raising of my hands like an evening oblation."*

After many years of praying the psalms, I'm starting to see the world through the psalmist's eyes: I see my daily life permeated with the saving presence of God, and see all of us as "children of the promise," waiting and working for the final victory of the kingdom. With the psalmist's eye, I see that my life and the lives of my brothers and sisters are chapters in the continuing story of God's loving care for all of creation.

We sit to sing the rest of the psalms of Vespers. Before long, a verse of Psalm 115 draws my attention: "*. . . House of Israel, trust in the* LORD; */ he is their help and their shield. / House of Aaron, trust in the* LORD *. . .*" But now, the words are no longer addressed to the "house of Israel": *Monks of Newark Abbey, trust in the Lord, He is your help and your shield.*

The chanted verses continue rising with the smoke of the incense: "*Those who fear the* LORD*, trust in the* LORD; */ he is their help and their shield. / The* LORD *remembers us, and he will bless us; / he will bless the house of Israel. / He will bless the house of Aaron.*" Once again, I hear the words of the psalmist speaking to us who are chanting them: *He will bless the house of Newark Abbey* as he did in 1973, when we were not quite sure if our little community would even survive.

The monks facing me on the other side of the choir take up the next verse, "*To you may the* LORD *grant increase, / to you and all your children.*" With the psalmist's help, I see the Lord watching over all of us monks and "all our children:" *To you may the Lord grant increase, to you monks and the hundreds of children who attend your school.* We're praying this afternoon that the Lord will continue to bless all of our children, from kindergartners to high school seniors, and bless our efforts to preach the Good News to them.

We continue chanting, "*May [we] be blest by the* LORD, */ the maker of heaven and earth.*" In the psalmist's view, God is the One who created us, the One who delivers us from evil, the One who listens to our prayers.

After a brief pause at the end of the psalm, the next psalm begins: "*I will thank the Lord with all my heart / in the meeting of the just and their assembly. / Great are the works of the Lord; / to be pondered by all who love them.*"

"*Great are the works of the Lord.*" King David, when he wrote those words, saw the hand of God acting in his own story and in the history of the chosen people, and of the whole world. Sharing his vision, I praise the "great works" that the Lord has done here on King Boulevard in downtown Newark.

The sweet-scented smoke, I notice, is still rising along with our prayers.

Reflection
Select a favorite psalm and reflect on it slowly, letting it speak to you personally, and ask what the message of the psalm might have to do with your life today. Some psalms to try might be Psalm 23 ("The Lord is my shepherd"), Psalm 51 (prayer of a repentant sinner), Psalm 91 (confidence in God), or Psalm 32 (prayer of a forgiven sinner).

Wednesday of the Third Week of Easter:
Dodgeball Players

Six kickballs whiz back and forth across the noisy gym. Several kids from both teams cower against the end walls of the gym, hoping to become invisible to the headhunters at the opposite end of the court, but an intrepid few go charging forward into the thick of battle, hurling balls to left and right with frightening velocity and reckless abandon. Then they whirl and jump and trip to avoid the dizzying barrage being fired back at them.

The players who charge forward are the ones who truly understand the game: win or lose, they dive in and take risks all the time, throwing their whole self into the effort—even if they are sometimes surprised by a painful smack in the head from enemy fire.

The spiritual life, which St. Irenaeus once called "a divine children's game," can indeed seem like a game of dodgeball at times: some of us, hoping to avoid dealing with the Almighty (whose involvement with us can resemble a barrage of kickballs), slither along the back wall, hoping to pass unnoticed by a God who is seeking us, who wants to enfold us in a loving embrace—and who, we suspect, will ask us to give ourselves entirely to him.

But sometimes the gift of grace comes along and mysteriously coaxes us away from the back wall, gently persuading us to take a risk; we are transformed from timid players, afraid of getting involved, into courageous contestants—into saints. Saints, you see, approach the game of relating with God by stepping up boldly, like some of the most daring students on the dodgeball court, and risk everything in the encounter with the Divine.

Francis of Assisi, for example, as a wealthy, charming and carefree young man, could hardly have been less interested in confronting God; then one day the Lord confronted him in a dream that challenged him to turn his life around. In response Francis took off all his clothes and left them in the town square and walked off, completely vulnerable before the Lord. He stepped into the center of the court and began dealing with everything the Lord could throw at him.

Benedict of Nursia, horrified at the decadence of Rome, gave up the life of a teenage schoolboy and set out, with just the clothes on his back, to give himself completely to confronting God one-on-one in the wild forests of Umbria.

A candidate came to the monastery door asking me if he could "try" the monastic life to see if it was for him. I warned him that you can't really "try it," with the attitude of someone dipping his toe into the pool before deciding to jump in. I suggested that he think of the monastic life as a dodgeball match: the best approach is to live it on the front line: encouraged by God's grace, and in the company of Benedict, Francis, and all the saints—and your community—you dash to the center of the court and start firing those big rubber balls as fast as you can, with everything you've got. You get bumped around. You get a bloody nose. A twisted ankle. But in the end, I told him, it's worth it. He believed me, I guess. He's been playing the game in his Benedictine habit for five years now.

Back in the gym, the dodgeball game has come down to a showdown between two wily players. Neither one looks ready to back down.

Reflection

Imagine that you are one of the players in the dodgeball game; which of their different approaches best characterizes your way of relating with God? Are you more like someone standing against the back wall of the gym, hoping not to get involved? Are you fearful and constantly on your guard? Or are you more like someone who embraces the situation and joins in with great abandon?

Thursday of the Third Week of Easter: *Charles*

Let me tell you about Charles.

I'm sitting with him in my classroom after school, listening to him talk about his absent father, his overbearing and unstable mother, and his failing grades in school. A single word keeps repeating itself in my head, like faint background noise at first: "victim." Then, as his list goes on, the word echoes more and more insistently: "Victim!" He complains, blames, and bemoans his fate. "VICTIM!"

At last I lose my patience and shout at him, "You know what? You're being a damned victim! You're choosing to be a victim of your absent father, your crazy mother, and of your crappy home situation! A guy with your brains has no excuse for failing all his subjects—especially my religion course!"

He stares at the floor, stunned by the force of my reaction. But I can tell he's listening, so I lighten up a little.

"I've just finished reading a book called *Deep Survival: Who Lives, Who Dies, and Why.*" I tell him about some of the individuals described in the book, most of them ordinary people who had survived in deadly situations while others around them had died. What kept all these people going was their "survivor mentality" even when the circumstances were completely against them. He's bright enough to figure out what this expression means—but he keeps his eyes on the floor.

"Charles, look at me! Thanks. Here's a question for you: What if you were to start seeing yourself not as a victim but as a survivor?" His expression slowly changes from shocked to quizzical. "I remember a simple sentence from the book: 'Survival is the celebration of choosing life over death.' It just seems to me that you can still decide to let go of your 'victim mentality' and choose to be a survivor instead." His expression goes from quizzical to curious.

"Would you like to borrow the book and read it?"

"Sure" (not enthusiastically).

Three months go by, and he never mentions the book I loaned him. Then one afternoon, as class periods were changing, he whispers to me in the hallway, "Father Al, I'm not a victim anymore." I quickly motion him to sit in an empty classroom. He tells me that he's getting all B's in his courses this semester, except for an A in algebra of which he's extra proud. He isn't quite sure, he says, how his change from victim to survivor happened, but he likes the way it feels.

"One of the things that helped me get started was that book you gave me. I read it, and I could really see myself in it."

I feel like jumping out of my chair, pumping my fist in the air and shouting "Yes!" But instead I smile in a calm, "priestly" way.

"Great! I thought it might help; I'm glad it did!"

I spend the three minutes before the next class reminding him that most survival stories aren't about instant transformation. The survivors in the book keep running into setbacks, and have to keep deliberately choosing life over death each time.

"You need to be ready for some of those setbacks yourself. And when they come, remember you've got a lot of people around here to talk to. You know I've got your back no matter what. Now we better get to class!"

"Thanks, Father Al; I'll remember." As he walks out into the hallway, I cross my fingers and say a quick prayer that he'll be able to stay as courageous as he is this afternoon.

Reflection

We are certainly subjected to all sorts of evils and difficulties in our lives. Think of ways in which faith in the risen Christ can help to overcome a "victim mentality."

Friday of the Third Week of Easter: *Birds*

Here's a story that I like to tell people—mostly because I need to keep hearing it myself.

After the Lord finished creating the animals, there was serious discontent among the birds. Watching the rabbits and cheetahs, they noticed how fast those animals could run. The birds were jealous, because the best they could manage was a painfully slow waddle or a series of short hops. Their problem was that they had to carry a sort of yoke on their shoulders: a pair of clumsy things that weighed them down and held them back.

Then, watching the trout and the bass, the birds noticed how gracefully and swiftly the fish could swim, and became jealous of them as well. Once again, the problem was the burden that the birds were dragging around on their backs, a weight that made it impossible for them to swim.

The birds got more and more depressed by their plight, until one day they decided to confront the Creator face-to-face. Thousands of birds went, all together, to complain to God that they thought it unfair that, because of the clumsy things they carried on their backs they could neither run fast, like rabbits and cheetahs, nor could they swim gracefully like the trout and the bass.

God listened patiently to their complaints, and then told them that he had something important to teach them. God invited them all to walk with him to the top of a nearby hill. They made a comical parade as they waddled and hopped, tripped, staggered and stumbled, following the Lord up the hillside.

When they finally arrived at the breezy hilltop, God told them all to face into the wind, and they did. Then God said, "Now, I will show you the secret about those burdens you're carrying on your backs, that keep you from running as swiftly as rabbits or swimming as gracefully as fish. I want you to spread those burdensome things out as wide as you can."

So the birds obediently spread their wings, and suddenly the strangest thing happened: their wings caught the wind and began to lift them off the ground. The birds started beating their wings up and down, until soon the sky was filled with countless birds soaring and swooping high above the fields and forests, speeding faster than the rabbits and cheetahs could run, and flying above the lakes as gracefully as any trout or bass could ever hope to swim.

To this day, the birds continue to fill the heavens with their songs of thanks to God.

Reflection

Think of something you consider a burden in your life. Is it possible that this is your "wings," and that you're mistaking it for a burden? Ask God to show you how you might use such wings, or how to open them to the uplifting power of God.

Saturday of the Third Week of Easter: *Nuno*

I'm standing at the counter of the Portuguese coffee shop, waiting for my espresso, when a friendly voice calls my name: "Hey! Father Albert! What are you doing here?"

I turn around to find myself face-to-face with a former student from some years ago.

I return his greeting: "Nuno! How've you been! What are you up to these days?" When the woman behind the counter delivers my espresso, he interrupts, "I've got this."

He hands me my cup and says, "Find us a table while I get my coffee."

I never liked Nuno, I think to myself as I sit at an empty table. He spent his four years of high school disrupting classes with his wisecracks, picking on smaller classmates, and studying just enough to get by—not to mention that I once caught him cheating on a test in my sophomore religion class. My musing is interrupted by Nuno, who is carrying a second cup of espresso and a plate with two golden yellow and brown Portuguese custard tarts.

As he sits down across from me, I have to admit to myself that despite my years-old negative feelings about him, I'm impressed by his spontaneous generosity, and at how fit and happy he looks in his neat long-sleeved shirt and tie.

He begins, hesitantly, "Father Al, I've been wanting to apologize for a few years, but haven't gotten around to it. So now, I want to say I'm sorry for giving you such a hard time when I had you in class." I try not to show my surprise as he continues, "But I've grown up a lot since then."

He pauses a moment, then continues, "That was almost nine years ago. Hard to believe." He seems to be reflecting, or considering what to say next. Curious, I decide to wait him out. "I bet you'd be surprised to know where I'm working now," he says proudly. "I'm teaching fifth grade. This is my third year, and I love it."

It takes a real effort for me to picture him in front of a class of fifth-graders. But, then, why not? Anyone can change.

Right now, I'm the one having trouble changing, letting go of my old opinion of him. Nine years ago, I comfortably relegated him to a box labeled "Problem kids I Have Taught," and haven't really thought much about him since. It's taking me some time this afternoon to let go of that prejudice. Meanwhile, he begins an impassioned description of his work as a teacher:

"I really love teaching. It's funny, but the kids I like the best are the ones who everyone else labels 'problem kids.'" Hmm, I think to myself, "Problem Kids I Have Taught" has a familiar ring.

"I guess maybe I understand them," he continues. "I remember how hard it was for me to just sit still and pay attention in school."

In a flash I realize that nine years ago, even on Nuno's worst days, God was loving him all the time, and in fact, was preparing him to be a good teacher who would know how to give special attention to kids who are like he once was. My old ideas about Nuno are quickly vanishing, as sunshine pours through the large windows, like Easter joy, brightening the whole café.

Then he says, "Hey! There's nothing worse than cold espresso." Neither of us has touched our coffee or our pastry. He lifts up his cup and makes a toast "*Salud!*—And thank you!"

"You're welcome!" I answer. As we down our cups together, I repeat to myself that anybody is able to change, including Nuno—and me.

Reflection

The Easter mystery is about transformation: from suffering to joy, from defeat to victory, from death to new life. The risen Lord is transforming each of us constantly; can you think of any ways in which he may have transformed you? Do you have a hard time letting go of your opinions and prejudices?

Fourth Week of Easter

Serving One Another

On the night before he died for us, the Good Shepherd, who laid down his life for his sheep, left us a commandment: *"Love one another as I have loved you,"* and told us, *"[As] I . . . have washed your feet, you also ought to wash one another's feet."* The meditations for this week, beginning with "Good Shepherd Sunday," remind us that the paschal mystery requires that we share not only in Christ's suffering and death and rising, but also in his generous self-sacrificing love.

This week's stories offer us examples of Christlike love in action, and remind us of the endless opportunities we have to be of service to others every day.

Fourth Sunday of Easter: *Sunday Preachers*

The people of St. Augustine's Church are always teaching me about Easter faith. Take last Sunday at eight-thirty Mass, for instance.

Standing at the lectern, I stretch my arms wide, trying to include everyone in a warm embrace, as I say, *"The Lord be with you."* In the moment that it takes to offer my greeting, I scan a wide swath of faces in this little inner-city church: a man in his thirties whose ravaged face betrays his ongoing battle with cocaine—I cringe with helplessness whenever I see Carl, since the only thing I can do for him is smile and call him by his first name when I give him a blessing. . . . A woman whose husband died a few months ago and who is wrestling with the horrible monster of grief—I wish I knew how to help her get through the pain, but all I can do is give her a priestly hug each Sunday, and a *"¿Cómo está usted, señora ?"*. . . . A husband and wife, heartsick because none of their grown children attend church anymore—all I can do is assure them that God loves their children and is certainly watching over them. . . . The woman who asked me last Sunday to pray for four of her relatives, each with some serious medical problem—I could only smile and promise to do so. . . .

I love these faith-filled people, each struggling to love the Lord and their families and neighbors as best they can. I sometimes wish I could be of some help to them in their struggles.

I look at my brothers and sisters as I read the gospel, proclaiming each of John's words carefully, as if these were the most important words they would ever hear: *"I am the good shepherd. The good shepherd lays down his life for the sheep."* To my left, Darnell, the homeless man who never misses a Sunday, sits staring at me, his head tilted to one side, as if he were carefully weighing every word.

"I am the good shepherd. I know my own and my own know me, just as the Father knows me and I know the Father. And I lay down my life for the sheep." In a front pew is a woman who burst into tears in the sacristy just before last Christmas as she told me that both she and her husband had been laid off, and so they couldn't afford to invite anyone to their house for the holidays—this woman is still holding on tenaciously to the image of the Good Shepherd who has been watching over her and her husband as they hunt for work.

As I end the reading with the traditional words, *"The Gospel of the Lord"* and everyone answers, *"Praise to you, Lord Jesus Christ,"* I suddenly feel humbled by the eloquent sermon that my brothers and sisters in the congregation are preaching to me this morning.

As they sit down, ready to hear the sermon, I realize that what they're looking for from me isn't practical help in solving their problems, but rather some words of encouragement to help them to continue trusting in the Lord in their trials and struggles.

Funny, I think to myself, that's the same sermon they've just preached to me.

Reflection

Think of someone close to you whose attitude and actions "preach" encouragement and hope to you. Do you think that this person knows that he or she does this for you? Do you think you do something similar for other people?

Monday of the Fourth Week of Easter: *Mike*

The soccer players are totally absorbed in their practice as I walk warily to the middle of the field, careful to avoid any stray shots. I say hi to the coach and then scan the field, trading waves with a few of my students as they run through their passing drill.

Then I notice Mike. Sitting by himself on the sideline in street clothes, a pair of aluminum crutches propped at his side, and a clumsy cast wrapped around his leg, he looks like someone marooned alone on a desert island.

I cross over toward Mike's island, aware of how great the distance between him and his practicing teammates must seem to him. When I ask, he mumbles dejectedly that he'll be out for six weeks. I advise him to do all his rehab exercises and he'll be fine. I can't believe how trite my words sound, so I stop talking and turn around toward the field.

The coach shouts encouragement to the kids nearest him, as a second coach, farther down the field, spurs his players on by calling them each by name: "Yes! Yes! Carlos, that's it! Much better! . . . Okay, Mario, now you've got it! . . . Nate, step into the ball. Yes! Well done! Good!" Some of the older players are also calling encouragingly to their teammates, telling them they're almost finished with the drill.

I glance over my shoulder to check on Mike, who is still sitting expressionless on his bench. I watch him for a moment and sympathize with him—I know what it feels like to be alone on an island of disappointment or dejection, when no one seems to realize that you're marooned there. My thoughts are interrupted by the coach calling "Okay, everybody, bring it in."

The exhausted players trot to the sideline to douse themselves with water from plastic bottles, and then, without so much as a nod toward Mike, hustle back to the middle of the field to form a loose knot around the coaches, as if drawing strength from standing close together.

If you've ever been in a situation like Mike's, you know that often even the people close to you seem so absorbed in their daily lives that they hardly notice you. Still standing on the side of the field, I remember remarking, as I was reading the Acts of the Apostles this morning, that St. Paul could strengthen his Christian communities simply by dropping in on them and being present beside them in their struggles.

A soccer ball wanders past me and rolls slowly toward Mike's island. I turn and see him, still slouched on the bench, poke at the ball half-heartedly with a crutch. Suddenly, it seems as if St. Paul is whispering to me, reminding me of the many times that I have been encouraged by someone's silent support; I walk over to the bench and, without a word, sit down beside Mike, sharing his island. We both stare straight ahead.

Reflection

Think of someone you know who is experiencing some sort of difficulty. As an "Easter person," how might you strengthen or encourage him or her? Can you think of other forms of encouragement besides words? Try recalling various ways that you have been encouraged by others, and ask the Lord to help you, in turn, to be a source of encouragement to others.

Tuesday of the Fourth Week of Easter: *Marvin*

"Just after daybreak, Jesus stood on the beach; but the disciples did not know that it was Jesus." (John 21:4)

I didn't know it was Jesus either. Not at first. But here's what happened. Someone at the front desk phoned my room and said that there was a man in the reception area who wanted to talk to a priest. I was "it."

"Good afternoon," I begin, as I walk into the lobby, "I'm Father Albert. What's your name?" The visitor, wearing a dirty hoodie and worn out sneakers, replies "Marvin, sir. I'm just looking to talk to a father. You a father, right?"

"Yes Marvin, I sure am." As we step through the doorway from the noisy reception area of the school and abbey and into the monastery, I take the direct approach right away:

"Okay, Marvin, I have to be up front with you: I can't give you any money. I don't have any."

"Oh, no, pastor. I don't want no money. Don't worry!" I don't really believe him, but I decide to hear him out. We sit in a little parlor.

"Thank you, pastor, for takin' the time to talk with me. I know you're busy, so I promise not to take too long. Well, I'll start with the fact that I was incarcerated for a year, and I been out since October—that's what, six months?

"I ain't gonna lie to you, I been strugglin' with drugs on and off for 'bout ten years. But I been clean for a month now. Trouble is, somewhere I used a dirty needle, so now I got HIV."

My compassionate side is starting to compete with my suspicious side, but a nagging voice inside me whispers "What does he want?"

"I got me a little job, cleaning up at a restaurant. It don't pay much, but hey, you know. Then my boss told me yesterday that he may have to lay me off because business is down. I'm just gettin' discouraged, you know?" His shoulders are slumping. A sliver of harsh sunlight cuts through the blinds and onto his tired, troubled face, making him look old, although he can't be more than about twenty-five; still, there's intelligence and kindness in his eyes.

"I'm afraid that with all these problems, I'm gonna start usin' again." Although his tone of voice is convincing, my own suspicious side reminds me that homeless people learn to be good actors. Then I notice a nasty purple welt under his left eye. That, I think, can't be very easy to fake. As he keeps pouring out his troubles to me, my compassionate side starts to win out.

I hear in my mind a prophetic line from Isaiah, sung in Handel's *Messiah*: "He was despised and rejected of men, a man of sorrows and acquainted with grief."

The "man of sorrows" himself is sitting right in front of me! It's taken me a few minutes to recognize him, but the disciples didn't recognize the risen Jesus right away either.

"So, I don't want to take up no more of your time, reverend. Like I said, I know you got things to do. All I want is for you to pray with me for a minute and say a blessing over me so that I won't go back on drugs, and that I can keep my job. That's all I need you to do."

"Well, that's something I'll be happy to do. Stay sitting for a minute." I stand up and extend both hands over Marvin, who once had crack in his veins and now has HIV. As I say a little prayer over him, I feel very strongly the grace of my "priest" role, but I feel just as strongly that I should be asking him for his blessing.

Reflection

We believe that Christ is present in every person we meet. In what sort of people do you find it easiest to recognize the presence of Jesus? In what people is it hardest to do so? Are there things you might do to help you recognize the Lord in the second group?

Wednesday of the Fourth Week of Easter: *Donors*

I smile at a woman who is standing at the curb in front of the monastery with a big bag of groceries at her feet; she looks me in the eye and says,

"God bless you! God bless you so much! This is wonderful!"

"I'm so happy you got what you needed! Let's pray for one another, okay?"

Our Pierre Toussaint Food Pantry is open this morning, and thirty men and women of various ages stand patiently in a line that moves slowly along the sidewalk in front of the monastery, and disappears through the door of the pantry. I say hello to an elderly woman,

"Morning, ma'am. How are you today?"

"I'm blessed!"

As poor as she is, needing to rely on other people's charity for food, she considers herself "blessed." I'm not sure my confidence in God would be any match for hers. Many of the people in line see their bag of food as a gift from the Lord, an answer to prayer from a God who takes care of those who call upon him.

They're right, of course, but in order to answer their prayers, the Lord works through other people. The canned goods and bags of rice and pasta are given by parishioners from suburban churches, by the members of our St. Mary's Church, and sometimes by the families of our students. So, the food comes from God by passing through the hands of generous donors. Which makes for an interesting twist: for most Americans, "the poor" is an abstraction referring to a faceless, anonymous mass. But in the food pantry, people walk through the door one at a time, and each is greeted with "Good morning! Could you please tell me your name? Each individual coming to the pantry is a person with a name and a face, someone who says, "God bless you so much!" or who returns a greeting by answering, "I'm blessed!" In an interesting kind of reversal, the anonymous ones in our food pantry are not the hungry individuals in the line, but rather the generous donors who have given the food that is being distributed.

Think of it this way. Jesus speaks somewhere about two different kinds of food. The first he calls "perishable food," the kind that people receive from the food pantry, and that is necessary for human survival. The second kind of nourishment he calls the "food that remains unto life eternal," and this, too, is distributed through the pantry: it is all the graces and blessings given by the Lord to each of the people who donate the first kind of food that fills the bags for their hungry brothers and sisters.

Whether providing physical bread for the hungry folks in the line at the food pantry or giving spiritual food to the generous donors, God knows each of them by name, and each of them can confidently say, "I'm blessed!"

Reflection

Do you see areas in your life where the risen Jesus works through you to accomplish good things such as helping people in need? What does this cooperation require of you in terms of effort, resources, etc.? What might "working for food that remains unto life eternal" mean for you in practical terms?

Thursday of the Fourth Week of Easter:
Lawrence

Lawrence, the student leader of my homeroom group, is serious about his job. Take the way he handled an eighth-grader in our group named Tyrone, who had been doing poorly in his classes, picking fights with classmates, and had recently begun coming late to school.

On his own, Lawrence, a senior, speaks with the youngster's teachers, looking for their advice as to how we might help him, then buttonholes Tyrone's best friend, Charles, and finally Mr. Crawford in the discipline office, but doesn't find a lot of suggestions for how we can help Tyrone. Nobody so far has found a way to get to him.

I'm impressed by the young leader's gentle, caring approach to this exasperating kid. I would ask "How can we make him behave?" but this high school senior is thinking first, "What can we do to help him?"

He's found out, though, that Tyrone's father was arrested again two weeks ago, and takes that as a good clue to what's really bothering him. So, Lawrence figures that Tyrone doesn't need people telling him stuff, but needs somebody to listen to him, and so the teenage leader is going to try sitting down with him himself. "The two of us get along pretty well, so maybe he'll talk to me."

I look at him and imagine I see Jesus kneeling to wash Simon Peter's feet. I ask myself, "What is my first reaction when I encounter a student who is being difficult? Is my first concern always the same as my young group leader's, to try to be of help to that student, to 'wash his feet'"?

I consider myself a good foot-washer, glad to help a parishioner who comes to me for spiritual help, and happy to help a brother monk who needs some help with a computer application—I'm good at serving people I like, and whom I think deserve my help. But with someone like Tyrone, who's difficult, uncooperative, and troublesome, my first reaction isn't always to ask how I might be of service to that person.

Watching Lawrence at work can certainly remind us that the life of an Easter person is mostly about washing people's feet.

Reflection

What are some opportunities that you have to be of service to others? Are there people whom it is difficult for you to approach with an attitude of humble service? Are you more comfortable when being of service to others than you are when someone is being of service to you?

Friday of the Fourth Week of Easter: *Sharonda*

Here's a story.

I'm on my daily walk, enjoying the sunshine and the gentle spring breeze, when I find myself on University Avenue, which is lined on both sides by the buildings of Rutgers Newark. I decide to rest for a few minutes before heading back to the monastery, so I find a bench facing the parade of students carrying books and backpacks along the crowded sidewalk. Taking out a couple of folded pages of a manuscript that I'm editing, I sit down and set to work, pencil in hand.

"'Scuse me, are you a professor?"

Startled, I look up to see a young woman staring at me expectantly.

"Not, really," I reply; "but I *am* a teacher." Curious now, I continue, "Why do you ask?"

"Well, I was wondering if you could go over my paper with me," she asks matter-of-factly, with the sweetest, sincerest smile ever. "It's due this afternoon."

Instantly charmed by her simple, trusting attitude, I reply without even thinking: "Sure! Have a seat!" (I mean, how could I say no?)

"Oh, thanks so much, really!" she says, as she plops down next to me, as relaxed and comfortable as if we were lifelong friends. As she opens her knapsack and pulls out some typewritten pages, she announces, "My name's Sharonda."

"Mine's Albert," I respond. "Nice to meet you, Sharonda. Now let's take a look at this paper."

Half an hour later, she stands and thanks me, then hurries off to type in her corrections. I get up and start to retrace my steps along University Avenue.

As I walk, I begin thinking what a remarkable person I've just met. Sharonda seems to assume that most people are basically decent and generous and willing to help someone in need—at least she felt free to walk up to me, a perfect stranger, and ask me to help her with her paper. I envy her optimistic outlook on her fellow humans.

Then I ask myself what it would be like to see people through Sharonda's eyes; I decide to give it a try. I continue walking, and whenever someone comes toward me on the sidewalk, I glance at the person's face and picture a brother or sister who would gladly help me if I asked for a favor. I'm amazed at how quickly and easily I begin to see goodness and beauty in each one of them. After the first three or four people, I also start to feel a connection forming between me and everyone I see; the connection is hard to describe, but it feels somehow familiar and warm and deeply human. People keep approaching and I keep sensing this mysterious, joyful energy flowing between me and each of them. This, I realize, must be what the poet John O'Donohue means when he asks God to "bless the space between us."

I wish I'd learned how to do this years ago, I think to myself.

See, we just never know when some Sharonda is going to come into our lives for half an hour and invite us to open our eyes to something beautiful that we've been missing.

Reflection

In Luke 17:21 Jesus tells us, *"The kingdom of God is among you,"* but this could easily be translated as *"the kingdom of God is* between *you,"* that is, in all the relationships you have with everyone in your life. What characterizes those "spaces" between you and your spouse, your coworkers, or the bus driver? Patience in one case, kindness in another, mutual encouragement in another: this is the kingdom. Are there any relationships, any "spaces" in your life that may need the healing touch of the risen Lord?

Saturday of the Fourth Week of Easter:
Three Witnesses

The Good News walks around our neighborhood all the time; and bumps into us when we least expect it. Take the guy pushing the wheelchair.

This man comes toward me hustling a wheelchair up the long hill toward King Boulevard, chatting away with his crippled, frowning passenger. As the hill gets longer and steeper, and the man in the seat gets heavier and his face longer, the pusher shortens his stride with a practiced ease that speaks of years of experience; he bends forward and says something that makes the man in the seat burst into laughter and forget for one joyful moment his useless legs. The chair floats past me and the rest of the way to the corner. I wonder what magical words the chair-pusher could have said to lighten his passenger's load and lift his spirits. He's Good News.

Or, how about this: I'm in the school office, watching the head of our middle school listen to a tinny voice spewing hot anger at her through the phone. Instead of hanging up on the rude parent, as I would have, she calmly responds as one mother to another, pouring the oil of understanding on the towering waves of rage and accusation, sympathizing with the upset mom, and asking, doesn't she find it hard raising a son all by herself? As if by magic, the screeching from the phone changes to a murmur as the two settle into sisterly commiseration about the unfathomably weird ways of twelve-year-old boys. In awe, I watch her living the Good News—being the Good News—for a sister.

Then there's what happened at a prayer service for a handful of homeless teenagers at Newark's Covenant House. A girl at our weekly chapel service asks if she can sing for us. She sits, eyes closed, and half-whispers her simple song: *"We fall down, and we get up. We fall down, and we get up. We fall down, and we get up . . . ."* The ten other homeless kids in the chapel sit mute at first, listening. Then, her ripples of pain begin to sound familiar to others; a bashful, breathy alto voice joins in, *"We fall down, and we get up . . . "* followed by a rough bass, grumbling slightly off-key, *"We fall down, and we get up . . . "* The three voices settle into the eloquent monotony that describes their lives: *"We fall down, and we get up . . . "* Then, like sudden sunshine bursting through a bank of storm clouds, a delicate, haunting soprano voice rises from the corner of the chapel—it's the new girl, Sylvia. Her song pours out a sweet, soothing balm, blessing and healing every heart in the room, including mine, with a beauty that comes from suffering, and wounds, and hard-won wisdom. *"We fall down, and we get up"* is no longer a boring repetition of futility, but the promise that no matter how many times we fall, we always end by getting back up. I ache with the poignant, infinite mystery of it all. She is not preaching the Good News, nor even singing the Good News, she is *being* the Good News. The rest of us fall silent and listen as she repeats the promise of the paschal mystery, *"We fall down, and we get up."* Sometimes the gospel hits us like that.

Reflection

Think of some people who serve as Good News for you. Do they do so by their words? Their deeds? Their attitude toward life? By simply being who they are? Are there people for whom you are Good News? How might you become a more effective bearer of the Good News?

Fifth Week of Easter

Walking in the Spirit

Christ's work of redemption is, as we've already said, not yet finished. To continue and complete his mission of saving the world, the risen Christ remains present and active in the church through the power of the Spirit, working in unseen ways in and through all of us every day. By sending the Holy Spirit on us, Christ made his work ours as well. *To each person the Spirit is given for some benefit* (see 1 Cor 12:7).

To enable us to be coworkers with him in his mission, Christ provides each of us with whatever gifts we need to bring it closer to completion. The stories this week celebrate some of the countless ways that we can show and share charity, joy, peace, and other gifts of the Spirit.

Fifth Sunday of Easter: *Gwendolyn*

If you open a window, be ready for the Spirit to blow right in. Here's a story.

As I stop at the traffic light at the corner of King Boulevard and West Kinney, a woman walks across the intersection toward me. She seems to be in her late twenties, but her haggard face and emaciated body make it difficult to tell. I always keep my car window rolled up when anyone approaches while I'm stopped at a light, but, for some reason, I roll it down as she walks up.

"Excuse me sir. Please, I'm trying to get me somethin' to eat; if you can spare a dollar or some change."

Since I can see that she really is hungry and in need of help, I say, "Let me pull over to the curb." As I drive across West Kinney, she trots after me and, when I park along the curb, she steps up to the window again.

"What's your name?" I ask.

"Gwendolyn."

"Well, Gwendolyn, I don't think I have any change, but let me see." She watches patiently as I search my pockets. I'm pleasantly surprised to discover three forgotten dollar bills, which I hand to her, saying,

"Hey, look at this, Gwendolyn! Didn't even know I had these. I hope they'll help."

As she accepts the gift, and (presumably noticing my Roman collar) says "Thank you reverend. God bless you."

"You're welcome, Gwendolyn," I respond. Then I add, "Please pray for me, okay?"

Imagine my surprise when, instead of promising to pray for me, she immediately folds her hands, bows her head, and, with eyes closed, begins to pray out loud right in the middle of the traffic on King Boulevard. She speaks as naturally and easily as if she were conversing with her best friend:

"Father Lord, I just thank you for letting this minister come along this way when I needed some help, Lord. Thank you for touching his heart this morning, and moving him to help someone in need." Her prayer immediately draws me in, and as I pray silently with her, I realize that she is giving me a glimpse into her heart—the humble, grateful heart of a woman who trusts completely in her Father's providence.

She continues, *"Bless him for being so generous, and make him a powerful messenger of your Gospel, Lord. Please anoint him with your Spirit, heavenly Father, and keep him strong and faithful in his work. In Jesus' name I pray."*

"Amen!" I respond quietly. "Thank you, Gwendolyn. That was beautiful."

After we exchange goodbyes, she turns and starts back toward the intersection, and I pull away from the curb, thankful for the gift I've just received: an encouraging example of intense, humble and heartfelt prayer.

I drive home keeping my window wide open.

Reflection

Think of a time when you received a gift from some "unlikely" person. Did that person know that he or she was giving you the gift? Do you think the Lord might be expecting you to pass on a certain gift to someone? Reflect on the image of "rolling down your window" to allow the Spirit to work in your life.

Monday of the Fifth Week of Easter:
Door Holders

The owner of the company that prints most of the abbey's and school's brochures and newsletters is showing me around his new facilities. He's especially proud of the great gray color-printing press that's loudly clacking out a river of printed pages as we stand watching.

When the foreman of that part of the shop comes over to greet us, the owner, who visited our school last month, introduces me as a teacher from St. Benedict's Prep. Then he immediately adds, enthusiastically, "You know what they do in that school? They hold doors for you. It's amazing!" He's genuinely enthused. At first, I'm sort of amused; then he continues, "I visited there last month, and these kids would stop and hold the door open for me. I didn't think kids did that anymore!" The foreman nods in agreement.

I'm pleased to hear that our kids actually did what we've been teaching them to do, and also that they made such a good impression on a visitor.

Holding doors is not an automatic reflex for most teenagers, who are often oblivious to their surroundings. So, I always take the trouble to call a student's attention to the fact that he has just let the door slam in my face. Many a time I've called a student back, saying, "Hey! Excuse me? Would you please come back in the door and try this again? Thanks. Now, this is how you hold the door for someone behind you." And, since good example is the best way of teaching, I and the rest of our staff usually make a habit of holding doors for students as well.

I don't contend, mind you, that holding a door for someone is fulfilling some biblical command or anything like that. But there certainly seems to be something important and valuable about the gesture. Why else would this president of a company be so impressed by our kids' habit? Could there be some deeper message behind such a simple gesture?

There's no gospel passage that records Jesus holding a door for someone and saying, "After you!" But I have no trouble imagining such a scene. He always seems extremely aware of the people around him, such as the blind Bartimaeus sitting by the side of the road, or Zacchaeus perched on a tree branch, or the paralytic lying alone at the edge of the pool of Bethesda.

I don't want to make too much of a simple act of kindness, but maybe the gentleman from the printing company sensed that holding a door for someone is an outward sign of an inner reality—which is the definition of a "sacrament," by the way. When someone who gets to the door before me pulls it open and steps aside and says, "After you," I sense the world is a slightly better place because of that person's simple, thoughtful deed, and my faith in the basic decency of people is renewed for a while.

Picture it: a world in which everyone holds the door for everyone else!

Reflection
"Being Christ for others" probably has less to do with imitating his heroic acts of self-sacrifice than with being as

aware of others as he was, and being as sensitive and responsive to their needs. Think of some person or persons who might benefit from more Christlike awareness on your part. What are some actions that you might take because of this awareness?

Tuesday of the Fifth Week of Easter: *Leo*

Leo, an alumnus from the '60s, stops on the concrete path that curves through the small landscaped area behind the monastery and school, and smiles as he looks around at the shaded green lawn, the neatly trimmed shrubs, the laurel bushes, and the bed of brilliant daffodils. Like most visitors, he says how surprised he is to find this quiet little oasis in the middle of the city, and how peaceful it feels. The songs of sparrows punctuate his comments.

I agree with Leo about the peacefulness of the little garden. As we follow the path together, I ask myself if he realizes that the notion of "peace" has a much deeper meaning than many people realize.

When I was a novice, my ideal of "monastic peace" was summarized in an image from a book by the Trappist monk, Thomas Merton, describing the sound of the monastery bells echoing across the silent, mist-shrouded hills of rural Kentucky. Since then, however, the experience of almost fifty years of living as a monk in the center of the city has considerably broadened and deepened my original idea of "peace."

Think about this: at the time when St. Benedict told his monks, *"Seek after peace, and pursue it,"* they were watching Roman civilization collapsing into chaos all around them; civil authority and public morality were disintegrating before their eyes, as marauding barbarians shut down commerce and communication. These first Benedictines must have figured out quickly that the "peace" Benedict was referring to had to lie deep beneath the chaotic surface of their lives, in some inner, spiritual dimension.

Benedict knew that Christ had given the gift of peace to his apostles—*"My peace I give to you"*—but the saint also understood that this gift requires some effort on our part to accept it and absorb it into our lives. So, the father of western monasticism included in his Rule for monks several practices that could help us lead a life of peace: humility, for instance, as well as silence, communal prayer, holy reading, and fraternal charity, to name a few.

Over the years I've certainly experienced that inner peace, but I've also learned how fleeting and fragile it can be. Sometimes, for example, while I'm meditating on a bench in this little garden, or even in front of the Blessed Sacrament at 5:00 in the morning, I'll experience the situation that St. Gregory describes with a humorous image: "The mind which is disordered by a rabble riot of thoughts suffers, as it were, from overpopulation." The noisy dialogue in my mind can completely overpower the gift of inner peace if I'm not careful. But, with the help of Sacred Scripture and the good example of my brother monks, I usually manage to calm the "rabble riot of thoughts" before too long.

As we continue along the path, I hope that the peace that Leo feels when walking on our grounds comes not only from the physical quiet, but from the peace that my brothers and I try to cultivate in our hearts, since that's our job as monks, to *"seek after peace, and pursue it."*

Reflection

The garden space is certainly soothing and calming and "peaceful." But Christ offers us another kind of peace "that the world cannot give"—one of the traditional gifts of the Holy Spirit. Think of some ways that you might cooperate with this gift "that passes all understanding": Is there, for example, a particular place or person or activity that usually leaves you open to receiving that gift of peace?

Wednesday of the Fifth Week of Easter: *Chain-Breakers*

Believe me, the energy and enthusiasm of 550 teenage boys lifting their voices in song will make your pulse race. At this morning's daily assembly in the small gymnasium, their powerful, joyful noise can be heard up on the fourth floor and over in the abbey church: *I always wanted me a hero! Now I got me a hero!* As the song gets underway, more and more voices join in: *Thank you Jesus! You're my Lord and King, You're my Lord and King.*[1]

The enthusiastic praise makes me think of one of my favorite scenes in the book of Acts: In the middle of the night, Paul and Silas, in prison in Philippi, are praying

---

1. Songs quoted in this chapter are by Peter Winstead (unpublished).

and singing hymns to God as their fellow prisoners listen; then, as they're singing, a powerful earthquake shakes the foundations of the jail, the doors fly open, and "the chains of all were pulled loose."

Students are singing who, I know, are living with chains every bit as heavy—and not as quickly broken—as those of Paul and Silas: an abusive parent, an addicted family member, numbing depression, seething anger. Some of our faculty members, and a few visiting parents standing in the corner might be suffering problems in their families or in other areas of their lives; they may not be singing, but you know they're praying along with us. Many of us, I suppose, are secretly hoping that a spiritual earthquake will come in the middle of our joyful shouting, like the Holy Spirit itself, to loosen all our chains.

Then a second gospel song begins; it's a little bit raucous, but its straightforward message can't be missed: *Don't give up! Don't give up! God has never lost a battle; Don't give up!* Many of the students, including freshmen sitting in neat rows on the floor, drape their arms over their classmates' shoulders on either side and sway back and forth in time to the music. The sophomore next to me puts his right arm over my shoulder, and soon I'm part of a long chain of swaying students singing, *Don't give up! Don't give up!* As the words of encouragement begin to sound like an Easter hymn, and the sounds of celebration grow even louder, I sense a special presence in the room: the healing power of community. As the kids link themselves into human chains of arms draped over shoulders, they are subtly lifting the weight of countless worries from one another's hearts and offering to share a bit of the struggle and pain that any brother in the human chain may be going through this morning. They sense unconsciously that, together, they're wielding a powerful if not-so-secret weapon against the powers of evil simply by loving one another. That's probably why they laugh and sing with such energy.

Okay, so maybe there won't be a real earthquake this morning, but this powerful sharing of loving community is certainly loosening some chains.

Reflection

If an inner earthquake were to surprise you, what chains in your heart or spirit might it break? Reflect on the effect of the presence of a community on your prayer: Does it make a difference? Why, or why not?

Thursday of the Fifth Week of Easter:
Children of Joy

As I walk across the soccer field on my way to class, I wade into a swirl of dozens of children from our elementary school who are running and playing tag during recess, filling the mild spring air with the sound of their laughter. Caught up in the spirit, I begin laughing along with them and returning their smiles. Since I'm a regular visitor to the first-grade classroom, many of the first-graders shout greetings. One of them, named Karim, who is missing a

front tooth, trots over to exchange a high five with me (a comical operation given the difference in our heights); a moment later I'm busily high-fiving first-graders with both hands amid shouts of delight.

I continue across the field, my spirits lifted on the surging tide of laughing children; finally, I turn and wave goodbye to them and head off to teach my sophomores today's lesson, on the kingdom of God.

Inside, a few minutes later, I see fifteen-year-old Brian struggling toward me down the long hallway, using his two metal walking sticks in place of his paralyzed legs. He passes between the two long rows of Penn Relays plaques, with bas-relief pictures of strong young athletes, trophies of triumphs in track and field, that line both walls. I feel so sad for this kid who's never run or jumped or climbed a fence, who'll never hike in the woods or play basketball, but will always have to watch from the sidelines. I wonder if he ever feels bitter about the unfairness of his situation. I think to myself that if I were in his place, I'd be furiously angry at God.

He interrupts my musing when he hobbles up and says hi. He shakes my hand with a grip of steel—a reminder that he's been using crutches his whole life. For some reason, maybe the way the light is shining, I suddenly see something in his expression that I hadn't noticed before: a mixture of serenity and acceptance. But as we talk, a certain look in his eyes suggests something deeper there than simple acceptance: a quiet joy. Not exuberant, over-the-top jubilation, but, rather, calm delight in being who he is and doing what he's doing. It seems that, because Brian has accepted the grace to be at peace with his cross, he is also experiencing the gift of joy.

Suddenly I remember a phrase from the first-century *Letter of Barnabas* that describes the early Christians as "children of joy." As I look at the expression on Brian's face, I ask myself if the first followers of Jesus really were recognizable as Christians by the look of joy on their faces and the joyful way they treated others.

And, if Brian's being a "child of joy" despite his handicap is remarkable, so is the fact that he passes on his gift, "the joy of the Lord," to everyone around him, including classmates and teachers and, right now, me.

Reflection
Jesus prayed for us at the Last Supper, *"that my joy may be in you, and that your joy may be complete."* What would being a "child of joy" mean in practical terms in your life? Think of some people who might benefit from your acting as a child of joy.

Friday of the Fifth Week of Easter:
The Spirit of Surprise

I smile whenever I think of the time the Holy Spirit caught us completely by surprise. It happened when our monastic community had been asked to consider adopting another small monastery, like our own, that was struggling to survive.

The discussion of the topic has been going along smoothly, and we've pretty much arrived at a consensus—namely, that there isn't anything that we, small in numbers as we are, can do to help that other monastery. "Let one of the bigger abbeys do it" we agree. Common sense has apparently won out, and it's just a matter of finalizing such practical thinking with a vote.

Then someone asks, "But when our community was in deep trouble in the early seventies, and things looked bad for us, didn't other monasteries step up and help us? Maybe it's our turn now to pass that help on to some other house."

I think to myself, "You know, he's absolutely right!" I glance around at my brothers, to discover that we're all looking at one another and evidently thinking the same thing. And another brother comments, as if to himself, "Well, that's true, we did get a lot of help from others when we needed it." Then someone else adds, "And let's be honest, we've been risk-takers ever since then, and God's blessed us each time we took a chance on doing the right thing."

Heads are nodding in agreement; the direction of the discussion has changed—as quickly as the breeze on a windy day.

Suddenly I start hearing in my mind the words of a song that we sing with our students, *"I can feel the Spirit movin', I can feel it movin'; I can feel the Spirit movin', I can feel it movin'. . ."*[2]

---

2. Song by Peter Winstead (unpublished).

One after another, we begin agreeing that maybe we ought to take the risk and let God figure out how we can be of support to the troubled community that is asking for our help. In the space of five minutes, all the prudent, sensible deliberations of the past half hour have gone out the window. When the question is called, the motion to adopt the other monastery passes easily, something no one would ever have predicted before the meeting.

As we walk out of the chapter room that morning, we ask one another jokingly, "What just happened in there anyway?"

I can definitely feel the Spirit moving.

Reflection

After the so-called "Council of Jerusalem" (Acts 15), the message that the apostles sent to the gentile Christians begins, *It is the decision of the Holy Spirit, and ours, too . . .* The apostles clearly felt that the Spirit had been at work in their community deliberations. Do you ever sense the presence of the Spirit in your life? If so, where? Do you ever notice the Spirit at work in other people?

Saturday of the Fifth Week of Easter: *Carl*

I really loved the students in my Third-Year French class that year—and hoped that I didn't show it too much. But when I told them I would miss class on Thursday and Friday to attend a conference, they cajoled me into bringing each of them a souvenir when I returned. (So much for their not knowing that they were my favorites!)

Back in class the next Monday, I walk around inside the circle of six desks and hand each kid, as promised, a souvenir of my trip to San Francisco—a keychain with a small plastic plaque at one end showing a cable car or the Golden Gate Bridge. The first five accept their gifts with a polite *"Merci beaucoup, Père!"* Until I get to Carl. He's one of my very favorite students ever, and is also a rabid fan of the San Francisco Forty-Niners. I'm pleased with myself for having remembered to get him a keychain that sports a logo of his beloved team. As I proudly stretch out my open palm and offer him the 'Niners keychain, I watch his expression. His eyes sparkle for a second, as a smile flashes briefly across his face. Then instantly his eyes cloud over; he frowns, looks down, and shakes his head, mumbling: "No thanks, I don't want it."

I'm caught by surprise and, to be honest, for a moment, I feel hurt by his refusal. His classmates alternately scold and coax him from all sides: *"C'mon, man. It's a gift!" "You can't refuse it . . ."* But Carl stubbornly withstands the barrage of impatient comments: *"Yo! It's just a damn keychain, Carl; just take it!" "What's your problem?"*

His frown betrays his dilemma: he doesn't want to offend me, and he doesn't want his classmates angry at him, but at the same time he obviously finds it difficult—maybe impossible—to accept the gift. I feel sad for him, and wonder what could be going on inside of him that makes it so hard to accept such a small present? The room falls silent as he stares down at his desk. We're at an impasse. I consider pulling the gift back and letting him off the hook, but my teacher's intuition—or maybe the Holy Spirit—tells me to keep my hand extended, quietly challenging him to accept the trinket. After fifteen seconds that seem like half an hour, he slowly lifts his eyes and stares at the keychain. I'm rooting hard for him: *C'mon Carl, you can do it!* My other hand is clenched nervously. Slowly, hesitantly, as if he were afraid it might bite him, Carl reaches out and plucks the present from my hand. The rest of us exhale. I suddenly realize that I've been holding my breath.

I don't know what it cost him to accept that little present—maybe accepting that gift was the hardest thing he'd ever done. Maybe the Lord used this small keychain to unlock a closed part of Carl's heart that day. And for this little Easter victory I say, *"Merci beaucoup, Père!"*

Reflection

The Lord stands in front of me, offering me in his open hand the gift of patience. What does he feel when I reject it, preferring instead to be furious with my brother monk? Does Jesus feel disappointed the way I did when my favorite kid refused to accept my keychain? I'm sure that he keeps his hand extended during the showdown, ready to outlast my stubbornness. And I bet that he exhales and sighs with relief each time I finally reach for the gift and say, *"Merci beaucoup!"*

Sixth Week of Easter

Unity in the Risen Christ

In his priestly prayer at the Last Supper, Jesus prays that all of us will be one in him as he and the Father are one. While making it clear that each of us needs to work toward achieving that unity, he also gives us the Spirit as a source of that oneness.

This week's meditations tell of how the Holy Spirit works in the people around us to help and encourage us, and to unify all of us in the communion of saints, uniting us with our brothers and sisters here on earth as well as with those who have gone before us into glory.

Sixth Sunday of Easter: *The New Brothers*

A large wooden plaque with raised letters hangs over the door between the school's reception area and the main hallway. Some woodworker sweated and sawed, carved and shaped and sanded each of those letters, wrestling and coaxing them from a plain wooden plank, and finally arranged them into our motto: *"Whatever hurts my brother hurts me!"*

The energy, effort, and skill that he put into making that sign, however, are nothing compared to the constant work that goes into getting kids to take the message seriously and live it. In a world splintered apart by hatred among national, ethnic, and religious groups, and in a country crackling with racial and religious tension and bigotry, the school motto is often as incomprehensible as Egyptian hieroglyphics to a new student.

Our freshman class is a widely diverse mixture of students of various skin colors, from different religions, language groups, and economic backgrounds, from cities and suburbs, from other states, and even from foreign countries. So, we pour a lot of effort and energy into helping them experience the truth of the brotherly motto, especially during the freshman orientation week, when they spend five days together at school sleeping on the gym floor at night, and spending their days going to class. During those days we use group exercises, team challenges, name games, peer tutoring, and anything else we can think of to challenge the new guys to adopt a whole new way of thinking: we're all in this together, our fates are interlocked, if a brother fails, that somehow hurts me as well.

During the entire week, the 140 freshmen, standing shoulder to shoulder in neat ranks and files, endlessly shout the school's motto: *"Whatever hurts my brother hurts me!"* The idea is that if they repeat it often enough, the motto,

along with countless shared challenges and other activities over the following months, will, like so many woodworkers' tools, eventually shape their hearts and minds, and influence the way they feel and act toward others. For more than forty years we've inspired students to think of those around him as their brothers, no matter how different from one another they may seem.

Over the course of their years in school, we ask them to reflect on variations of the motto, such as *"Whatever helps my brother helps me,"* or *"Whatever hurts me hurts my brother."* To accept any of these convictions involves a long process of conversion for many of us, adults as well as students, and requires constant recommitment and reinforcement.

The motto carved out of pieces of wood is the first thing our students see each morning. We hope that by the time they graduate, they will no longer need the sign, but will carry the conviction in their hearts: *"Whatever hurts my brother hurts me!"*

Reflection

Think about Paul's words to the Corinthians, *"that there may be no dissension within the body, but the members may have the same care for one another. If one member suffers, all suffer together with it"* (1 Cor 12:25-26). What is your first response to this text, or to the motto, "Whatever hurts my brother hurts me?" In what sense do you believe it? Would you put qualifications on it? Do you belong to any groups that seem to live by this motto? We sometimes ask our students to reflect on some variation of the motto, such as "Whatever helps my brother helps me," or "Whatever hurts me hurts my brother." Reflect on how these sayings might apply to your life.

Monday of the Sixth Week of Easter:
Peter Miller

Here's a story to ponder. I heard it from a brother monk at supper. During the American Revolutionary War this guy named Michael Wittman is captured and at his trial is proven to be a turncoat who has often given the British invaluable assistance. He is found guilty of spying and sentenced to death by hanging. On the evening before the execution, an old man with white hair asks to see General Washington, giving his name as Peter Miller. Since this Miller has done a lot of favors for the revolutionary army, he is ushered in right away. This time, however, Miller is about to turn the tables by asking for a favor from Washington. After the general greets him cordially, Miller gets directly to the point, and shocks the general out of his chair by asking him to pardon Michael Wittman, the notorious turncoat. Washington is baffled and surprised by Miller's plea, and explains that to grant his request would be impossible. Wittman had done everything he could to betray his fellow colonists, even offering to join the British to help destroy Washington and his army. Shaking his head, the general apologizes, "In these times we cannot be lenient with traitors; and for that reason, I cannot pardon your friend." "Friend!" cries Peter Miller, "He's no friend of mine. He is my bitterest enemy. He has persecuted me for years. He has even beaten me and spit in my face, knowing full well that I would not strike back. Michael Wittman is no friend of mine!"

Washington is puzzled. "And you still wish me to pardon him?"

"I do. I ask it of you as a personal favor."

"Why?"

"I ask it because Jesus did as much for me."

Washington turns away and walks into the next room. Soon he returns with a paper on which is written the pardon of Michael Wittman. "My dear friend," he says, placing the paper in the old man's hand, "I thank you for this."

I can understand that Michael Wittman might have been grateful to his enemy for arranging his pardon, but here's General Washington, who has just been imposed upon in the worst way, thanking the man who has imposed on him. It just goes to show you: you never know how your actions are going to help someone else. Miller hadn't set out to teach Washington anything, but his example of unflinching commitment to his religious principles turned out to be an unintended gift to a harried general in the midst of the ugly carnage of war.

To be honest, I don't know if I would have Peter Miller's strength of character if I were in his shoes. But I do know that I have had a couple of Michael Wittmans in my life whom I needed to forgive, and I surely have been pardoned by people whom I've hurt. I've even been in General Washington's place, too, being edified by someone else's example of courage or gentleness or forgiveness. What's always going to remain hidden from me, though, is the number of times that I have unknowingly helped a brother or sister by my good example—simply by acting like Peter Miller and doing what I thought was the right thing.

Reflection

Reflect on a time that someone forgave you for something you had done. What do you think their motivation might have been? Reflect on how you felt when you heard that you'd been forgiven. Have you ever had the opportunity to forgive someone? Reflect on Peter Miller's depth of faith, and how real must have been his own experience of God's forgiveness.

Tuesday of the Sixth Week of Easter: *Soccer Fans*

Cries of dismay burst from the nearby tables: the French World Cup team has just scored a goal. One or two men shout at the television screen mounted above the open-air bar, in the parking lot of the Iberia Restaurant. With school on summer break, I've walked down the hill from the monastery in time to claim a table under the warm July sun, and catch the 10:00 game being broadcast on a Spanish cable channel. For the price of a cup of coffee I get to watch not only the World Cup match between France and Mexico on the television, but also the people around me. The men and women at the next table, dressed in Mexico's green, white, and red, are quietly focused on the figures on the television screen.

Having spent many pleasant months in France, I'm rooting for the French team, but I keep a prudent silence and enjoy the good-natured cheering and banner-waving of the Mexican fans sitting all around me.

Here in this multiethnic neighborhood, the World Cup stirs up passionate emotions that sometimes show themselves in shouting, hooting, and loud groaning directed at the television screen. As I sit here surrounded by green, white, and red flags and soccer shirts and the sounds of different languages, I realize that I'm part of a single group of close to one billion brothers and sisters around the world watching this game or listening to it on the radio. Each national group is rooting for its own team, certainly, but just as importantly, they are all united by a common passion for soccer.

This morning I celebrated Mass for the Missionaries of Charity in their convent chapel. The congregation was made up of sisters from around the world: India, Brazil, the United States, Costa Rica, and Canada. When we prayed the Our Father together in all those different accents, the word "Our" took on a wide, sweeping meaning. The "we" gathered around the altar extended far beyond the walls of the convent, and out past the boundaries of city, state, and country to embrace everyone in the world. The word "Our" was not the "we" of "us against them" that you find at a soccer game, but a "we" that proclaims our belief that all of us are children of the same loving Father. When "we" is used that way, it challenges us to break out of our closed little circles of self and realize that the only way we can truly pray with Christ is as members of the great "we" of his kingdom, where there are no walls, no divisions or prejudices or animosities.

Mexico misses a corner kick, and all my Mexican brothers and sisters groan. Without thinking, I groan along with them.

Reflection

When do you have a strong sense of belonging to a "we," a group with which you identify? Do you find it easy or difficult to imagine yourself as a sister or brother to members of all the ethnic and religious groups in the world?

Wednesday of the Sixth Week of Easter:
We, the Branches

I pause on my walk through the Spanish-Portuguese neighborhood to study the grape arbor at the corner of Elm and McWhorter.

Lush leaves are already stretching halfway across the overhead wires in long bunches, like tousled green caterpillars. The branches seem to be filling out right before my eyes as they burst with new life, sprouting shoots and tendrils in every direction. The arbor is lifting its head and hands and praising the Lord, as the gnarled vine stocks, as thick as small tree trunks, send raw, vital energy through the branches, to the farthest end of the arbor.

I immediately think of the image that Jesus used at the Last Supper, telling his apostles that he is the vine, and they are the branches; he doesn't say that he is the vine and they are the grapes. No, they are the branches, the lush, vital, growing part of the vine, a crucial element in the ongoing life of the plant. Then he tells his apostles: *"My Father is glorified by this, that you bear much fruit."* My goal as a Christian can't be simply to become a branch that is lush with leaves, any more than one of these branches I'm looking at is meant to produce nothing but leaves. My purpose is the same as that of every branch in this arbor—think of the heavy clusters of dark purple grapes that will be hanging from these branches in the middle of September.

Doesn't grace flow like sap, from Christ, the vine stock, into us Christians, who are the branches? And don't we, then, turn it into different kinds of fruit—into a kind word, say, or a helping hand, a generous gesture, or a gentle response to an angry word? And doesn't Jesus say that this is how we will be known and judged—by our fruit?

I start to picture my monastic community as a lush grape arbor springing from a single stock, and made up of fourteen different branches. Sometimes we get in one another's way, sometimes one branch irritates another by rubbing against it too hard. But somehow, in the end, we manage to help one another glorify the Lord of the harvest by "bearing much fruit."

Reflection

Jesus says, "I am the vine, you are the branches." In what way(s) do you experience the truth of this statement? Think of some group or groups of which you are a member. Do any of them seem like vines from which you, as a branch, draw life, or which enable you to "bear fruit?" What are some fruits that Jesus may be expecting you to produce right now?

Thursday of the Sixth Week of Easter:
Community of Believers

In church before Morning Prayer, I'm meditating on Acts 4:32 (NABRE): *"The community of believers was of one heart and mind."* The commentary that I'm reading on this passage declares, "Luke's portrait of this first community is obviously idealized."[1] The portrait may be idealized, I say to myself, but it's not impossible—I once experienced a community that was of one heart and one mind right here in this monastery.

As you may remember, that was back in 1972, the year during which our school was closed. My mind wanders back to that time of pain and uncertainty. Having experienced together the painful closing of our prep school and the transfer of half of our brothers to another monastery six months before, the thirteen of us who had remained had the sense, at first, of being a group of survivors sharing a lifeboat. But, as we faced together the challenges of an unknown future, we quickly developed a bond of mutual

1. Luke Timothy Johnson, *The Acts of the Apostles*, Sacra Pagina series, ed. Daniel J. Harrington (Collegeville, MN: Liturgical Press, 1992), 61.

trust. By December we were already discussing how we might open a new, smaller school in our empty buildings.

I'll always remember the feeling of community in the small circle we formed one snowy morning as we began to shape the future school. We took turns telling each other about our individual strengths and weaknesses as teachers, as well as our hopes for the new school. The bond of mutual trust in the room grew; the snow fell steadily.

Back in church, I'm startled when my book starts to slide off my lap, and my eye is drawn back to the Scripture verse, *"The community of believers was of one heart and mind."* When I think again about that sense of unity we shared forty-four years ago, the description of the early church in Acts really doesn't seem so far-fetched at all.

Then I notice that, immediately after giving the idealized picture of the Christian community, Luke, the author of Acts, begins telling of disputes and difficulties that began to crop up in the church—which is why the commentator says that "one in mind and heart" is an idealized description of the reality. I suppose my own memories of that meeting in 1972 are an idealized picture as well—I'm sure that we had to work our way through plenty of disagreements, but after forty-four years, I've forgotten those arguments. Like Luke's recollections of the early church community—which were fifty years old by the time he wrote Acts—my recollections are, by now, I admit, pretty thoroughly idealized.

Suddenly, I realize that the close, loving community that we experienced over forty years ago in the midst of our trials and doubts, was a rare gift from the Lord. And, even if the gift fades with time into ordinary Christian fellowship, we, like the author of Acts, need to keep telling the story among ourselves to keep us from getting satisfied with our present community life. And we need to tell the story to everyone we meet, so that they, too, can marvel at the wonderful works the Lord has done.

Reflection
The Acts of the Apostles presents an idealized picture of the life of the early Christian church: *"The community of believers was of one heart and mind"* (Acts 4:32). Think of some of the communities to which you belong. Are any of them blessed with a sense of oneness? What might make you less (or more) willing to make the effort needed to foster the unity of that community?

Friday of the Sixth Week of Easter:
Neighborhood Helpers

The long room that serves as living room, dining area, and kitchen of this first-floor apartment needs painting, and the furniture is threadbare, but everything is clean and well cared for. Ninety-three-year old Marta and I have walked from church after Sunday Mass, past several vacant lots to the only house left on the block, to bring Holy Communion to her sister, Elena, who is sitting back in a big armchair with a blanket covering her lap.

After the short but reverent ceremony is finished, Marta asks, *"Padrecito, quiere tomar un cafecito?"* Since this isn't really a question ("Would you like a cup of coffee?"), but a request for me to stay and visit for a few minutes, I accept her offer and sit facing Elena while Marta, following the tradition of her biblical namesake, bustles off into the kitchen area at the far end of the room.

I ask Elena to tell me what it was like when she was a little girl growing up in Puerto Rico. Her eyes grow bright as she lifts her head to look at me, and starts reminiscing easily about life on the family's tiny farm. Whenever she pronounces the words *"la finca,"* "the farm," the words have a rich, magical overtone. When the farm stopped being profitable, they had to move to New York. Then come the sad tales of their mother's sudden death, their father's unemployment, their brother's drug addiction, and the family scraping by without simple necessities. The little apartment where we are now sitting shows that they've never won the battle against poverty. I begin to wonder how the two sisters have managed to keep going into their nineties despite all their hardships.

Then I notice that everywhere on the walls there are pictures of various saints, men and women, as well as recent popes: some of the images are in frames, but many are obviously cut from magazines or calendars and taped to the walls. There is an old crucifix, too—and, of course, a statue of the Blessed Mother.

Suddenly I realize that, in this, the only house left on the block, these pictures of saints and religious statues make up the sisters' neighborhood, filled with the holiest and kindest of neighbors, who watch over them and intercede for them with God. Looking around now with the eyes of Marta and Elena, I see the room as a comforting refuge.

I glance up at the big picture of the Sacred Heart of Jesus above the television and realize that, through this picture Jesus keeps encouraging the sisters amid their struggles, just as he did Paul during his night in prison, with the message, "Keep up your courage!"

I look around again at the crucifix and the circle of saints gazing down on us, and imagine them, on days when things are at their worst, whispering, like helpful neighbors, comforting words to Elena and Marta.

Definitely a special neighborhood!

Reflection

Reflect on the idea that the risen Jesus is *always* in your neighborhood.

The letter to the Hebrews encourages us, *"since we are surrounded by so great a cloud of witnesses, . . . let us run with perseverance the race that is set before us"* (Heb 12:1).

Reflect on some of your relatives and friends who have gone before you into glory, and how they are now not just watching you but encouraging you to run the race with perseverance. Think of those for whom you may be an important "witness," a source of encouragement to them as they run their race.

Saturday of the Sixth Week of Easter:
Thirsty Neighbors

Here's a living parable, a scene so powerful and thought-provoking that you may think I'm making it up.

I've just driven through the entrance gate and onto the spacious grounds of the Benedictine abbey of San Antonio Abad, located on the eastern coast of Puerto Rico. As I search for signs of the severe drought that is afflicting the island, I notice, at the side of the road, several people standing near some cars parked in a stony little parking area, watching a young man lift large plastic water containers into the trunk of an old sedan. Curious to find out what's going on, I slow down to watch. At the other end of the parking area, several people are gathered around a stone retaining wall built into the hillside. They're standing in line, waiting to fill containers from a pipe that protrudes from the face of a stone wall. I say to myself, "How cool is that! During this drought, local people are coming to the monastery to get water!" I continue driving up the winding road toward the monastery, delighting in the vivid image of thirsty neighbors streaming to the monastery to receive such a precious gift from the monks.

This is what monks do—we don't normally leave our monastery to go out to help people, but rather we welcome our neighbors who come to us for help. In downtown Newark, for example, although we have no spring of water to share with thirsty neighbors, we have other gifts that draw to our monastery people with all kinds of needs. Parents bring their children to us to study in our school. Worshippers fill the abbey church each Sunday, others come to our daily community Eucharist or Vespers, and still others ask for spiritual guidance. Some of our poorer neighbors come to the food pantry for groceries, and street people come to our door looking for something to eat—or for a kind word of blessing or encouragement.

Like the cool water flowing from the pipe at San Antonio Abad, all the gifts that we offer to people have been given to us by God, and we, like our Puerto Rican brothers, simply share our gifts with everyone who comes to our monastery.

Reflection

The monks of San Antonio Abad pass on to their thirsty neighbors the gift of water. Think of some gifts that God has given you. Do you share them or make use of them to benefit others? What is one gift that you might pass on to someone who needs it?

Seventh Week of Easter

Glimpses of Light

We Easter people live in the "in-between time" between the "already" of Christ's resurrection and the "not yet" of his final coming to bring the kingdom of love to fulfillment.

As we keep working courageously to move the world toward that goal, we are encouraged from time to time, as the chapters of this final week describe, by delightful glimpses of the fullness that will surely be ours one day.

Seventh Sunday of Easter: *Freshmen Rowers*

The freshmen stand at attention along the dock, fidgeting silently while the coach assigns each of them a seat in one of the two eight-man boats moored beside them. As each steps gingerly into his place in one of the long narrow boats—some of them for the first time—he concentrates on not tipping it over or putting his foot through the bottom. All of them are too busy to notice the afternoon sun shimmering silver on the river, or the schools of wind ripples chasing each other under the bridge in crazy zigzags.

As each new rower sits down awkwardly and grips the oar at his chest, he knows almost nothing of the exacting skill and coordination it will take to push back in his seat while putting that oar in the water at exactly the correct angle and pulling with just the right amount of strength, and then rotating his wrists to the correct angle so as to lift the oar out of the water smoothly, with no splashes—all of this at the same time as the rest of his crewmates.

He'll soon learn that the goal is for every member of the crew to function in perfect coordination with the rest, everyone doing exactly the same thing the same way at exactly the same time. When all eight members are rowing perfectly together like that, it's called "swing." A boat gets its swing only when each member leaves his own concerns behind on

the dock, including his physical discomfort and his personal problems, so as to become one with the rest of the "eight." As each individual forgets his pain for the time being and just pulls, they begin to pull as one, and the boat starts flying through the water. It's hard to get to that point, though. Many rowers feel swing only once or twice, if ever; and just for a minute or two, because it's hard to hold on to swing.

Swing is a parable of what happens in a good community. I've felt it among my brothers in the monastery a few times, when every monk puts aside his ego, his personal projects and wishes, and gives up what he wants for the sake of the group.

The other day, when we were singing Vespers, I noticed that all the monks on my side of choir were chanting effortlessly, with one single voice, at the same pace and the same volume, with exactly the same inflections. We were praising the Lord with our swing. And I've felt it in our community meetings, too, when we were wrestling with some important issue, and the brothers started listening to one another and letting themselves be persuaded, so that we came to a unanimous decision. Sometimes during our evening recreation period, when the novices and some of us other monks play cards or simply sit and talk together, there's a delightful hint of swing in the room.

Standing on the dock this afternoon, as I wave to the two beginner boats gliding tentatively away from the dock and setting off slowly up the river, I silently wish each of the new oarsmen a practice filled with the awesome rhythm of swing—and a life filled with the same.

Reflection

In the Holy Rule, St. Benedict gives his monks advice on how to work together in community as we work toward our common goal of heaven: "They should each try to be the first to show respect to the other, supporting with the greatest patience one another's weaknesses . . . No one is to pursue what he judges better for himself, but instead, what he judges better for someone else. . . . Let them prefer nothing whatever to Christ, and may he bring us all together to everlasting life" (72.4-5, 7, 11-12).[1]

Have you ever experienced swing as a member of a family, a group, or a community? If so, what was the experience like? What did you need to do as a member of the group to make the swing possible? Think of a situation involving others where you might contribute more to the unity of the group.

Monday of the Seventh Week of Easter:
All the Nations

Another day is beginning, as all our days begin in the monastery, with the familiar solemnity of 6:00 a.m. Vigils. We begin by chanting the refrain of Psalm 66, repeating it after every few verses sung by the cantor: *"Let the peoples praise you, O God, / let all the peoples praise you"*—words which I've

1. Timothy Fry, ed., *The Rule of Saint Benedict 1980* (Collegeville, MN: Liturgical Press, 1981).

sung thousands of times over the years: *"Let the peoples praise you, O God, / let all the peoples praise you"!*

I settle into the routine, carried along on the gentle swell of the fourteen voices of the rest of my brothers. *"Let the peoples praise you, O God, / let all the peoples praise you"!*

Suddenly, the familiar morning mantra seems to take on a surprising new life, the quiet mood gives way to a feeling of energy. We've been asking God to let "all the peoples" join us in praising the Lord, and now, without warning, I have the feeling that "all the peoples" are indeed praying with us right here, in the abbey church, and that we're now worshipping with millions of Palestinians and Jews, Muslims and Christians, Hindus and Buddhists: *"Let the peoples praise you, O God . . ."*

Each time we repeat the refrain I sense more deeply the unseen presence of untold millions of people who do not even know Jesus, but who are loved and embraced by God, and are saved by Christ's death and resurrection. I imagine myself joining all these peoples in praying with a single voice for peace around the globe, especially in the countless countries where, every day, members of rival national, racial, and religious groups try to destroy one another. Then, I pray for our country, where religious intolerance and racial hatred divide many of us and poison our hearts.

The cantor chants the final line of the psalm: *"May God still give us his blessing, / that all the ends of the earth may revere him"!* As we sing the refrain for the last time, and I imagine our voices louder than ever: *"let all the peoples praise you,"* I think of Isaiah's vision of the future heavenly banquet: *"On this mountain the* LORD *of hosts will make for all peoples / a feast of rich food, a feast of well-aged wines . . ."*

The opening psalm concluded, my brothers and I sit down and begin to pray the rest of the psalms of Vigils. We are only fifteen voices once again, but I still feel as if I'm seated at that crowded banquet table with "all the peoples," and I realize that what we prayed for this morning in Psalm 66 is also what God hopes for—what the Lord intends to accomplish eventually through us: that all the peoples of the world will, indeed, one day worship together on that holy mountain.

Vigils returns to its usual rhythm, accompanied by the familiar early morning traffic noises of cars and buses. A bird on a branch in the garden sings through the open window behind me, enthusiastically chirping the psalm with us.

Another day is beginning . . . and the world goes on—only, now, with the prayers not only of our little community of monks. The world goes on with the prayers of all the nations.

Reflection

As you pray Psalm 96:7, *"you families of peoples / give the* LORD *glory,"* imagine yourself praying not only with millions of Christians and Jews, but also with countless millions of people who do not know Jesus. Try to sense that all of them are your sisters and brothers in Christ, each known personally to God, and redeemed by the death and resurrection of Christ. Imagine the sound of a chorus, singing in hundreds of languages and in a rich variety of voices. How do you feel as you join in the song?

Tuesday of the Seventh Week: *Abraham Pierson*

Here's a tale that is worth retelling. In 1666, Robert Treat and his band of Connecticut Puritans have founded Newark as a theocracy—only members of the church can vote or participate in the city's civic life—an arrangement that will last for eighty years. After a long discussion about choosing a name for their new town, a prominent early settler, Abraham Pierson, suggests that it should be named after the English city, Newark-on-Trent, where he once served as a preacher. As heads nod their approval, however, he proposes, in addition, that, "in order to reflect the new task at hand," the town's name should be spelled "New Ark," that is, "New Ark of the Covenant."

The first part of his proposal is accepted, and the name "Newark" is officially adopted. But the second part, that it be spelled "New Ark," is rejected. Although for the next hundred years some citizens will still be spelling the name of their city "New Ark," Abraham Pierson's visionary name, "New Ark of the Covenant" will eventually be completely forgotten.

Pierson's idea deserves a better fate—there is deep wisdom in naming the colony a new ark of the covenant. In the book of Exodus, the ark, a rectangular box containing the two stone tablets of the commandments, is a constant reminder of the covenant the Israelites made with the Lord. More to the point for Pearson, the ark is the place where God shows himself present with this people as they wander in the wilderness: it goes at the head of the column of marching Israelites, guiding them through the desert, and protecting them from danger. The newly established town will be a place where God will be present, and will challenge the chosen people to be faithful to the covenant.

For Christians, the ark finds its fulfillment in Christ, who is God's presence living among us, protecting us and guiding us, the New Israel, through the wilderness of our day.

But, St. Benedict teaches that Christ is present in every person we meet, whether the very young, the very old, the poor, the sick, the abbot, or a fellow monk. This means, then, that each one of us is an ark of the covenant—a new ark of the covenant.

When I walk the streets of downtown Newark, I see people in business suits, flowing African robes, Bermuda shorts, and blue jeans, bustling beside women carrying shopping bags, teenagers wearing headphones, senior citizens leaning on canes, and mothers holding toddlers by the hand. I look for the face of Christ in each of them. And, remembering Abraham Pierson, I sense that the risen Jesus is present in all these brothers and sisters, as he is everywhere in this city, in this "New Ark" of the covenant.

Reflection

St. Benedict seems to base his Rule on two fundamental presuppositions: first, that God is present in every place, and, second, that Christ is present in every person. Do you experience one of these two principles more easily than the other? How might you make use of one or both in your efforts to live the gospel?

Wednesday of the Seventh Week of Easter: *Cartwheel Kid*

Picture this. About a block from home, nearing the end of my daily walk, I notice four kids who seem to be a family, walking past the monastery, coming in my direction. Even from this distance I can hear Big Sister practicing a loud football cheerleader shout, as three-year-old Little Sister jumps and hops along beside her. Behind them, teenage Older Brother bops down the street, with four-year-old Tiny Brother taking quick little steps to keep up. They all stop at the corner of King Boulevard and Springfield, waiting for the green light, with Big Sister clearly in charge, even as she continues to practice urging on her invisible team with a loud, enthusiastic cheer. When the light changes, they start across King Boulevard.

Suddenly, for no apparent reason, Older Brother, who is halfway across, throws himself into a stunning cartwheel—with arms and legs stretched perfectly straight, he is transformed, for two magical seconds, into a shiny spinning bicycle wheel. He finishes the cartwheel, and slips smoothly back into full walking stride, bopping to the other curb next to Tiny Brother, who doesn't seem the least bit surprised at his brother's freewheeling way of crossing the street.

I burst into the widest smile ever, delighted with the surprise, and marveling at the carefree, spontaneous exuberance of Older Brother. I say to myself, if that's how I felt when I saw his cartwheel, imagine how God must have felt—the One who created this boy, and gave him those supple arms and legs, and filled his soul with dance music.

I wonder if God doesn't delight in watching all children do cartwheels in the crosswalk, take their first steps, learn to ride a bike, or solve algebra equations.

We Christians, you know, come from a long line of gymnastic ancestors. King David is the best example—a cartwheeling king who leapt and danced before the Lord in the procession of the ark of the covenant. The book of Proverbs tells us that when Wisdom was helping the Lord create the world, she danced before him. At the end of time, the book of Revelation promises us, all of creation will rejoice together, delighting and rejoicing before God's presence. Just picture it: all of us, from every age and nation, shouting cheers for God, the way Big Sister does for her invisible football team, or bopping to celestial music together—and maybe even doing occasional perfect, spontaneous cartwheels in the crosswalks of heaven.

Reflection

Creatures praise the Lord in countless other ways besides words. For example, trees praise God by growing tall and spreading leafy branches to the heavens. Humans have traditionally danced and used other bodily gestures. Can you think of some other ways in which you praise God and, perhaps spontaneously, show your joy in the Lord?

Thursday of the Seventh Week of Easter:
Heavenly Cooks

Protected from the hot August sunshine under a great white tent, and fanned out across dozens of tables, two hundred or so people are eating and conversing. The bright colors of the tablecloths are as varied as the guests sitting around them enjoying "Monkfest," our monastery's annual family picnic. Students and their families, alumni, friends, neighbors of the abbey, and monks' relatives and friends form a group composed of members of various races, economic backgrounds, languages, and religions.

Guests wait patiently in line at the separate food tent, where a buffet table is loaded with dozens of bowls, platters, and casseroles. Off in a corner of the big field clouds of white smoke billow from the hot dogs and hamburgers on the grill. Behind me, people crowd around the beverage table, its bright orange coolers full of iced tea and lemonade, promising some relief against the heat.

Multi-hued banners flutter from the high fences in the warm breeze, while Frisbees and soccer balls sail above the wide lawn, and children are having their faces painted at one end of the big picnic tent.

A woman carrying a platter covered with aluminum foil enters through the wide-open gate and heads to the "Food

Drop Off" sign—all the picnic dishes are brought by the people themselves, and everybody gets to taste the different foods from different countries. Fried chicken, curried rice, potato salad, cut-up fruit, empanadas, meat pies, and maybe some goat meat—we never know from year to year what surprises will appear on the buffet line.

Several people are relaxing on blankets under trees as the school's pep band entertains from the lawn in front of the residence hall. I notice a group sitting on the lawn eating while listening to the music, and I immediately think of the crowd in the gospel story that was seated on the grass when Jesus multiplied the loaves and fishes.

As I look around me at the wonderful variety of people at our picnic, I understand why the gospel writers saw in Christ's feeding of the crowd a sign of the future heavenly banquet. The Monkfest, a celebration of community and peace among four hundred people of different backgrounds and from different parts of the world, is a real acting out of Isaiah's prophecy of people from diverse nations gathering on God's holy mountain at the end time for a great feast. The Monkfest, however, is different from the heavenly feast in one important way: here, everyone shows up bringing something to contribute to the meal. Some guests can only afford a small box of donuts, while others bring large platters of chicken. (I'm sure that some of those platters represent a real sacrifice on the cook's part.)

Suddenly, I smile as I imagine this scene: all of these good people of different races and religions, rich and poor, showing up by the hundreds at the heavenly banquet the way they come to the Monkfest, bringing big bowls of potato salad, plates of Spanish chorizo sausage, casseroles of mac and cheese, aluminum trays of collard greens, and big red platters of fried chicken; they ask St. Peter to point them to the "food drop-off table."

Reflection

The Monkfest is a joyful reminder to each of us to begin getting in practice for the heavenly feast by building up one another here on earth every day through our kind deeds and loving words, and by breaking down walls of suspicion and hatred. Reflect on how you are building up the kingdom on earth. Can you think of any walls of suspicion or enmity in your life? If so, you might ask the Lord to help you to get rid of them.

Friday of the Seventh Week of Easter: *The Garden Lady*

When it comes time to redo the cloister garden, one morning a man drives in on a little Bobcat tractor with a mechanical shovel on the front, and scrapes off a thick layer of grass and weeds, like a giant peeling an orange. It's hard to watch as the machine rudely uproots familiar hedges and shrubs, every last one, and the man and his helper lift the Blessed Virgin from her concrete pedestal in the center and lean her against a wall. From there she presides mutely over the proceedings as her garden is scratched into a big scar of soil, dusty stones, snips of roots, and shards of branches bleaching in the June sun.

Our pet cat surveys the catastrophe from beneath a wheelbarrow, dismayed that his familiar home has suddenly become a desert of dirt, bordered with remnants of weeds, bits of strangled hedges, and wisps of wilted grass. I sympathize with the poor animal.

Next afternoon this lady in Bermuda shorts and a wide-brimmed straw hat appears holding a clipboard; she stands in the center of the new wasteland, slowly surveying it with a practiced eye. Watching through a closed window, I become totally engrossed as she pantomimes to the brother monk in charge of the project, drawing expansive sweeps with her arms, carefully pointing to the exact places where phantom flower beds and planters belong, and slicing with her clipboard the nonexistent path of slates leading down the center to the future location of the statue of the Virgin Mary.

For the woman in the straw hat, this is not a patch of dirt, but a patch of possibilities and promises. I swear, she can see the new garden already spread at her feet, as real as the dirt she's standing on. Which is some trick, when you think about it.

Sometimes you stand in the middle of a messy situation, horrified at the hopeless havoc that some man in a Bobcat tractor has wreaked. You keep staring, but all you see is a chaos of clods and yanked-up roots, and piles of worn-down slates torn from old pathways. There's no guarantee that you'll ever get to see beyond the chaos, but you stand there and hope, and wait, and trust.

And sometimes, amid the messiness, the Lord will offer you a fleeting glimpse of a small piece of the garden. It may come when someone does an act of kindness for you, for example, or when a loved one warms your heart with a smile, or maybe when the rising sun slants upward through pink clouds in a splash of breathtaking glory. These tiny hints, sparkling splinters of the unspeakable beauty of the garden, help us develop the same kind of vision that the lady in the Bermudas and the straw hat has; we, too, can begin to see with the eyes of Easter faith: instead of a patch of dirt, a patch of possibilities and promises spreads at our feet, as real as the dirt we stand on. Which is some trick, when you think about it.

Reflection

Even if the complete shape of God's loving plan is hidden from us, it seems that the Lord encourages us with occasional glimpses of heaven's glory. Can you think of an instance in which you saw a ray of heavenly joy shining through some experience or some person? If so, what was your reaction to the experience? Do you think that the Lord ever uses you to offer someone a glimpse of heaven's love or joy?

Saturday of the Seventh Week of Easter: *Circus People*

According to an article in this morning's newspaper, Ringling Brothers, Barnum & Bailey Circus is going out of business. I'm sure that the news will sadden millions of circus-lovers, who will miss the clowns, the acrobats, and the trained animals, but I'm going to miss something else: the excitement of the circus' arriving in town.

Every year, a couple of days before the opening performance, a procession of colorful circus wagons, trailers, and trucks would arrive, and park in the streets around Newark's Prudential Center, just down the hill from the monastery. Several house trailers, a few low tents and countless bales of hay would take over the parking lot. Then, after the final performance, all the wagons, trailers, tents, and trucks would vanish overnight. The next morning, the streets and the parking lot would look the way they had before the circus had arrived.

This is why I've always thought of circus people as kindred spirits to us monks: they live "on the road" for several months a year, literally pulling up stakes every few days and moving on to somewhere new, like perpetual pilgrims. And "perpetual pilgrim" has a familiar ring to me as a Benedictine monk, since our monastic community is a band of pilgrims on a long journey together toward what St. Benedict calls "the tent of the kingdom." Everything about the monastic life is designed to remind us that we are on the road. Our vow of poverty keeps us from accumulating a lot of material possessions; our vows of celibacy and obedience witness to our belief that there is more to life than what we perceive with our senses. We don't intend to settle down here, because there's more, there's so much more, in our true home beyond this life.

In the Prologue to his Rule, Benedict tells his monks,

"Clothed then with faith and the performance of good works, let us set out on this way, with the Gospel for our guide, that we may deserve to see him who has called us to his kingdom.

If we wish to dwell in the tent of this kingdom, we will never arrive unless we run there by doing good deeds" (Prol. 21–22).

We monks, along with our families, loved ones, neighbors and friends, are wayfarers on the journey to the kingdom.

Now that our kindred spirits, the pilgrim people of the circus, will no longer be coming to town every year to remind everyone that we are all living on the road, our witness as monks will be even more important. We'll have to be sure that we are living in a way that reminds everyone around us that this world is not our permanent home, and that, like those people from Barnum & Bailey's Circus performing for a few days in Newark, all of us are just passing through.

Reflection

All of us Christians are always on the road, like circus people, traveling through life as the pilgrim people of God. Jesus told his apostles, *"You do not belong to the world"* (John 15:19), in other words, don't get too settled in, too satisfied, but live as if you were only passing through this present world. If someone were to look at the way you live, would one get the sense that you are a pilgrim on the road to somewhere beyond the present world?

Pentecost Sunday

Pentecost People

"When they had prayed, the place in which they were gathered together was shaken." (Acts 4:31)

So, maybe you think that Luke is exaggerating when he describes what happened to the first Christians in Jerusalem: *"When they had prayed, the place in which they were gathered together was shaken."*

Well, I think he's probably describing the scene exactly as he witnessed it—having myself felt a few church buildings almost stagger and shiver with powerful surges of shouts of praise. Take, for instance, the 10:30 Mass last Pentecost Sunday.

Although Mass has ended, and the celebrant has left the sanctuary of the abbey church, most members of the congregation show no sign of wanting to stop singing at the end of the recessional hymn, "The Strife is O'er"—which was chosen, I suppose, because this celebration marks the end of the Easter season. The leader of song directs the choir to repeat the triple shout, *Alleluia, alleluia, alleluia!*

She speeds up the tempo a little at each repetition, and we keep singing faster and louder each time, urged on by the full organ, a tambourine, an African drum, and a three-foot long cowbell. Everyone in the church seems to feel the Spirit uniting us as we sing the *Alleluias* with a single voice.

As I look at the people around me, though, I realize that there's more going on here than just Christians making a joyful noise. The Spirit, after all, doesn't descend on the church just to liven up the music—the Spirit always comes on business, you might say, with some greater purpose. Those Christians in Jerusalem, we're told, *"were filled with the Holy Spirit and spoke the word of God with boldness."* Notice that the Spirit gives them exactly the gift they need at the moment, namely, the courage to keep on preaching the Word despite setbacks, failures, and persecution.

I can imagine the gifts of the Spirit, prophesied by Isaiah, swirling through the church this Pentecost morning, whirling in different directions, each one hovering like a tongue of fire over anyone who needs some particular help.

I can almost feel Wisdom pour down on a single mother trying to raise her headstrong daughter into a good Christian adult. I can easily imagine Courage descending in several places: on the father sitting toward the back who's just lost his job; on a woman with a walker, and on a parishioner singing in the front row, who told me how hard he struggles to pay his bills. I imagine Understanding shining like sunlight onto the hearts of a newlywed couple in the third row, who were married here just two weeks ago. The teenagers from the youth group, who like to sit together, are probably flooded with the gift of Right Judgment pouring onto each of them. I'm not sure which gift the Spirit is sending me, but I'm hoping for a bit of Knowledge of God's unfathomable ways.

The organist opens every stop, and the choir and many of the people in the congregation keep up the joyful shout that can be heard a block away. And I feel the way some of those first Christians must have felt when *"they had prayed, the place in which they were gathered together was shaken; and they were all filled with the Holy Spirit."*

It seems as if the river of Easter fire that poured from the paschal candle and out of the church during the Easter Vigil and flowed all through the city, is pouring back in through every window and door.

Can you think of a better way to end the Easter season?

Reflection

If the Holy Spirit gives each of us the gifts we need, what might be a gift that you would ask of the Lord today?

Epilogue

Now, with Pentecost Sunday we've come to the end of our journey through the Easter season. I hope that you've enjoyed meeting the people with whom we have discovered various aspects of the paschal mystery in our everyday lives. You may well have recognized some of them from having already met them yourself—with different names and different faces, of course.

I hope that reading these stories will encourage all of us to continue discovering signs of the Easter mystery unfolding today and every day of the year.

And so, now, may the risen Lord keep walking with us on our homeward journey, and continue showing us more and more his presence in the lives of the sisters and brothers whom we meet on the way.